CW01429279

THIS BOOK

was first published in 1821 by Samuel Yates of Congleton. This new edition had been entirely reset in Garamond Narrow 11 point by Christine Pemberton and has a foreword by Stephen J Sebire M.B.E. and an introduction by John Condliffe.

The edition is limited to 500 numbered copies.

This is copy no ....**376**....

© The Silk Press Ltd 2000
ISBN 1 902685 05 9

HISTORY
OF
THE ANCIENT TOWN
AND BOROUGH
OF
CONGLETON

By

SAMUEL YATES

With Illusrations

The Silk Press
2000

FOREWORD

Over the years the town of Congleton has faced many challenges. As we enter a new millennium we find ourselves, yet again, going through one of those challenging times. The manufacturing industries are becoming more capital intensive and employing less people, whereas the new service industries are now seeing a period of extensive growth.

Taken as a whole the town offers a wide range of benefits, with many opportunities for the townspeople to participate in the considerable number of excellent facilities available to them.

Yates's 'History of Congleton' stands as an enduring memento of our past and will, perhaps, provide the reader with the opportunity to dream about our heritage and the present and future challenges we face.

We are indebted to the Silk Press for the painstaking way they have republished this rare and interesting edition, finally making it available to a wider readership.

Stephen J Sebire, M.B.E.
Chairman, Congleton Chamber of Commerce

INTRODUCTION
John Condliffe

I was pleased to hear that Samuel Yates's 'An history of the Ancient Town and Borough of Congleton' was to be reprinted 180 years after its original publication, thus making it available to a wider readership.

Few people in Congleton possess a copy, and such is its rarity that during my 50-plus years with the 'Congleton Chronicle', 30 of them as Editor and thus much involved in local history, while original copies of Robert Head's 'Congleton Past and Present' and the more recent Stephens's 'History of Congleton' have come 'onto the market' from time to time, I can remember only one copy of Yates's book being offered for sale.

Yates was, of course, Congleton's first local historian, his book of 1820 predating all others, thus being a valuable and much quoted source of information for those who followed.

He was obviously a remarkable man, much involved in the town's affairs outside his busy business life.

He was one of the local industrialists and businessmen who financed the town's gas works.

And it may not be generally known that he was much involved with the Congleton Trustee Savings Bank on its establishment in 1819, and which still flourishes today, albeit later having moved next door to its own premises and become part of the T.S.B. national organisation, and, more recently, Lloyds T.S.B.

He was its secretary and treasurer, (these posts were subsequently crossed out and the title 'Actuary' substituted), its trustees deciding in 1828 that he should be allowed £50 a year for those duties.

He was given another £10 for the use of his room, "with fire, candles and other things necessary for the use of the bank".

And there, it might be said, he and I have something in common, because the bank trustees met for a few years in a downstairs room of the Town Hall, but then, for the next 23 years, in Yates's printing works, stationery shop and dwellinghouse at 11 High Street, which is where the 'Chronicle' was founded in 1893, where it is still published today, and of which, like him, I am now the proprietor.

It is possible that I am sitting where he sat over a century and a half ago, writing about local history just as he did, the difference being, of course, that I now do it on a computer network, whereas he would be using a quill pen!

I suspect, however, that my office was the main front room of his Georgian dwellinghouse, still possessing the original firegrate from which he, no doubt, got his warmth until his death in 1833.

Perhaps the antiquity of the building, which still retains much of its originality, encouraged him in his interest in local history. It is certainly the oldest building in the town with a continuous use in the same field of business — a pamphlet printed in 1887, with an illustration of the premises, and the name 'S. Yates, Bookseller' over the door, states that its use as a bookselling and printing establishment had been traced back 150 years even then, which takes us back to the early 1700s.

If such an influence is possible, then it had the same affect on one of his successors there, Robert Head, founder and first Editor of the 'Chronicle' and writer of the second history of the town. Robert's son Lionel, who succeeded him as Editor, had a similar deep interest, contributing much valuable information to the 'Chronicle' files, and I hope it can be said that I have done the same, and that my son Jeremy, who has succeeded me as Editor, (just as Lionel Head succeeded his father) will keep up the tradition started by Samuel Yates in a building in which both the town's early histories were written, printed and published.

AN HISTORY
OF
THE ANCIENT TOWN AND BOROUGH
OF
CONGLETON

WITH AN APPENDIX,
CONTAINING
A BRIEF HISTORY AND DESCRIPTION OF
Astbury Church
AND BIOGRAPHICAL SKETCHES OF
EMINENT NATIVES.
COMPILED FROM THE MOST AUTHENTIC SOURCES
By

SAMUEL YATES
CONGLETON

*Printed by and for S. Yates, High-Street,
and sold by him and different booksellers in Cheshire;
also by Longman, Hurst, Rees, Orme, and Brown,
Paternoster Row, London
M.DCCC.XX.*

TO

RANDLE WILBRAHAM, ESQ.

HIGH-STEWARD OF CONGLETON.

SIR,

PERMIT me to inscribe this volume to you, as a public testimony of my esteem and respect, not only for your strict impartiality in the high official situation you hold in this corporation, but for the many virtues which adorn your private character. In this sentiment, Sir, I am convinced that I shall meet the approbation of my fellow-townsmen, who have long experienced the good effects of your temperate, yet firm and manly defence of their municipal privileges; your attention to their general prosperity as a body; and your urbanity to many of them as individuals.

I have the honor to be,

    Sir,

    Your obliged

    and very humble servant,

                    SAMUEL YATES.

                    CONGLETON,

                    Jan. 3d, 1820.

SUBSCRIBERS

A

ACKERS, George, esq. Roe Park,
Antrobus, Sir Edmund bart. London.
Antrobus, Mrs.
Acton, Mr.
Alsop, George esq. Uttoxeter,
Andrew, Mr.
Andrew, Mr. John jun.
B.
Banks, Mr.
Barker, Mrs.
Barlow, Mr. Thomas,
Barlow, Mr. Paul,
Barlow, Mr. George,
Barlow, Mr. Charles,
Barlow, Rev. Luke,
Berry, Mr. Belle Vue,
Bladon, Mr. Joseph, Uttoxeter,
Bladon, Miss Eliz. ditto,
Bond. — esq. Birmingham,
Bonney, Rev. George, Sandon, 2 copies.
Booth, Mr. Allen,
Booth, Mr. William,
Booth, Mr. Thomas,
Booth, Mr. Thomas, west-street,
Booth, Mr., market-place,
Boyse, Mr. Samuel,
Boughey, Mr. John,
Bostock, Francis, esq.
Bostock, Mr., Newcastle,

Bridges, Mr.
Broadhurst, Mr. James, Mosley hall,
Brougham, Mr. Burslem,
Braithwaite, Mr., Macclesfield,
Broadhurst, Mr. John,
Broad, Mr. Thomas,
Brown, Mr. James,
Brown, Mr. William,
Bradburn, Mr.
Bull, Mr.
Bull, Mr. George,
Buckley, Mr. Robert,
Buckley, Mr. Henry.
C.
Capper, Mr,
Castley, James esq. Rugeley,
Chaddock, Mr.
Cliffe, Mr. William,
Cockram, Mr. Thomas,
Copeland, Mr. Scholar Green,
Cookson, Mr. George,
Cooper, J. esq. London,
Cotton Mr.
Cowlishaw, Mr.
Cox, Mr.
D.
Darcy, Rev. John, Marton,
Dakin, Mr.
Davenport, Mr. Daneinshaw
Drakeford, Mr. William,
Drakeford, Mr. Edward,

Duff, Mr.
E
Edwards, Mr.
F.
Ferrers, the Right Hon. the Earl of,
Fillingham, Rev. John,
Foden, Mr.
Foden, Mr. Edward,
Ford, Mr.
Ford, Mr. James,
Ford, Mr. William,
Forster, Mr. Joseph,
Forster, Mr. John.
G.
Galley, Mr.
Garside, Mr.
Gee, Mr. William,
Gent, Mr. Charles,
Gent, Mr. Peter,
Ginders, — esq. Ingestrie,
Ginders, Mr.
Goodall, Mr.
Goodwin, Mr.
H.
Hadfield, Mr.
Hall, Mr. surgeon,
Hall, Mr. Thomas,
Hackett, Mr.
Harrison, Mrs.
Harrison, Mr.
Harwar, Mr.

Haywood, Mr. William,
Heath, Mr. William,
Henshaw, Mr.
Henshaw, Mrs.
Hickton, Mr.
Hilditch, Rev. John, Leafields,
Hilditch, Miss, ditto,
Hilditch, Mr. Bechton house,
Hirons, Mr. Thomas,
Hogg, Mr. Near Daneinshaw,
Hordern, Mr.
Hutton, Mr. Thomas.
J.
Johnson, John esq.
Johnson Mr. Joseph,
Johnson, Mr. William,
Johnson, Mr. Throstles Nest,
Johnson, Mr. Near Daneinshaw,
Johnson, Miss Jane,
Johnson, Mr. James.
K.
Keeling Mr.
Knight, Mrs. London,
Knight, Mr. Edward, Tunstall.
L.
Lowndes, William, esq. 2 copies,
Lowndes, William, esq. Endon,
Lowndes, Mr. John, 2 copies,
Lawrence, Miss, Windfield hall,
Leadbeater, Mr. Thomas,
Low, Mr. Surgeon,

Lowe, Mr. Charles.
M.
Machin, Mr. Burslem,
Madders, Mr.
Malbon, William, esq. Dane Bank,
Marshall, Rev. William, Macclesfield,
Meek, Miss,   .
Moorhouse, Mr.
Morris, Mr.
Norbury, Mr. Charles,
Norbury, Mr. London,
Oakes, Mr.
P
Pattison, Nathaniel Maxey, esq.
Platt, Mr.
Parsons, Mr. John,
Partington, Mr.
Pedley, Mr. William,
Pike, Mr. John,
Porter, Mr. Astbury,
Potts, Mr. William,
Poynton, Mr. Peter,
Piggot, Mr. Moreton,
Procter, Mr.
R.
Reade, Mr. John, chapel-street,
Reade, Mr. Moss,
Redfern, Mrs.
Robinson, Mr. John,
Roe Mrs., west-street,
Roe, Mr. Charles,

Rowley, Mr. James,
Rogers, — esq., Birmingham,
S.
Skerratt, Mr. Marsh,
Skilbeck, Mr.
Sherratt, Mr. Charles,
Shaw, Mr. John,
Smallwood, Mr.
Smith, Mr.
Smith, Mr. John,
Smith, Miss,
Smith, Mr. Amerton,
Staton, Mr.
Steele, Mr. Burslem,
Stringer, Mr.
Stubbs, Mr. Peter,
Swetenham, Clement, esq., Somerford Booths,
Swetenham, Miss, Moody house,
Sutton, Mr. Isaac.
T.
Tamworth, Viscount,
Thorley, Mr.
Thornicroft, Miss, Moreton,
Toddington, Mr.
Townley, Mr.
Twemlow, Mr.
W.
Wilbraham, Randle, esq., Rode hall,
Wilbraham, Randle, esq. jun. ditto,
Watson, Holland, esq.
Wilson, Rev. Edward,

Walley, Mr.
Waller, Mr. James,
Wallworth, Mr.
Webb, Mr. Buglawton,
Wilkinson, Mr.
Woolfenden, Mr.
Wood, Mr.
Worrall, Mr. Ishmael,
Wright, Mr.

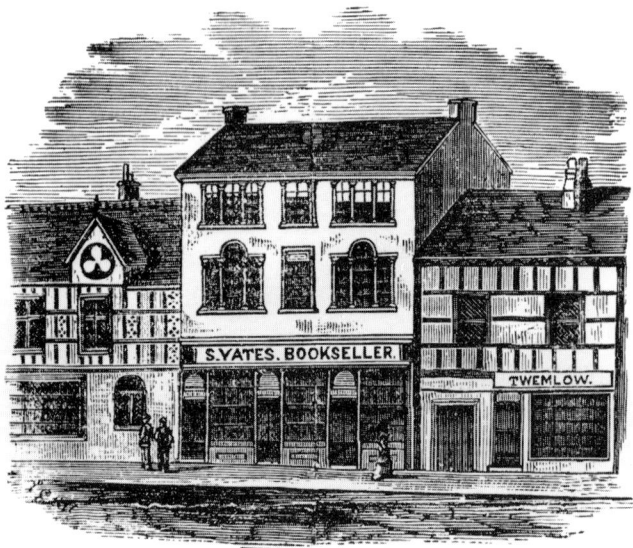

"Ye Olde Congleton Boke Shopp"

This is an illustration from a faded pen and ink drawing made probably early in the present century. The existence of the prominent building in the sketch as a bookselling and printing establishment is traced back upwards of 150 years, and is said to have been founded by two maiden ladies. Here it was the venerable Samuel Yates, sixty years ago, lived, and wrote the first (and as late as the present year, the only) History of Congleton, which has long since been out of print.

The structural alterations necessitated by time have robbed Congleton street architecture of many quaint old houses, and the two on either side of our illustration have long since disappeared, but the old "Boke Shopp" retains much of its originality.

(Pamphlet printed in 1887)

Engraving courtesy John Condliffe

PREFACE

A COMPREHENSIVE HISTORY OF CONGLETON, from the earliest recorded period of its existence, to the present year, 1820, is now respectfully offered by the author to his numerous subscribers, and the general reader. If a satisfactory account of this ancient borough had been published, the author would never have undertaken the task of compilation; but convinced as he is, that all former descriptions of the town are very imperfect, and induced by facility of access to the corporation records, and the advice and aid of intelligent friends who favored him with their observations on the subject, he has produced this small topographical work, which he hopes will prove pleasing to his townsmen and the public in general.

The transactions of any community during seven centuries and a half, must, when faithfully recorded, afford rational gratification to the human mind; for what can be more interesting than an authentic history of the gradual progression of society from its rude origin, ignorance, and indigence, to a flourishing population enjoying all the benefits of intelligence, opulence, and refinement? Such the compiler trusts, his history of this ancient borough will be found, and however defective it may appear to the fastidious critic, when considered as a mere literary composition, it still must possess a high claim to the attention of the natives and residents of

Congleton, and every individual who wishes to possess an authentic and amusing record of this beautiful and prosperous town.

Perhaps no topographical work was ever produced under happier auspices, for the compiler, not only had permission from the municipal officers of the borough to make extracts from the corporation books, but he also received the treasured collection of an observant townsmen, who had taken notes of all remarkable occurrences in the town and neighbourhood during the last fifty years. As a resident himself, the author can plead no excuse for any errors in the topographical part of the work, for the descriptions are the result of actual observation. Thus his sources of information respecting the ancient, as well as the modern state of Congleton, were not only genuine but ample. On the former subject, the antiquary will find much important matter, especially the charter granted to the borough by Henry Lacy in the twelfth century. Exemplifications of the charters granted by successive sovereigns to the corporation, are printed in chronological order, and a correct abstract of the ample charter of James the second, which forms the basis of the franchises of the borough. Curious extracts from the records of the town are also given, and present many instructive and entertaining illustrations of the progressive improvements made in the useful arts and civilization in this town during the lapse of nearly three centuries.

A retrospective view of the improvement of Congleton, since the erection of the first silk-mill, and a brief history of the introduction of the spinning of cotton, and the influence of these two branches of British manufactures on the population, wealth, and morals of this community, will doubtless afford much information to the man of business, and furnish some hints to the writer on national wealth, and political aggrandizement. Indeed, the rapid accessions of population, commercial wealth, and profuse luxury in the manufacturing counties, present a political phenomenon which seems to baffle and confuse the most acute writers on the subject. Good and evil will spring up together in the best civil institutions, from the natural imperfection of man; yet when we behold the glorious and successful efforts of philanthropy to promote human happiness; when we see such numbers of our youth of both sexes brought up in habits of honest industry, and instructed in the true principles of religion and morality, we may confidently aver, that opulence contributes to the general good of the community while thus employed in the service of benevolence. This will appear completely illustrated in the description of those excellent institutions which have been founded in this town during the present age.

Such are the general subjects described in this volume, throughout which the compiler has steadily adhered to truth, and endeavored to unite amusement and utility. He therefore hopes that his well-intended exertions will meet with the approbation of every liberal and impartial mind.

It now remains for him to express his acknowledgments to well-informed individuals for the aid which they afforded him in his compilation. Among these he must first mention his friend Mr. WILLIAM JOHNSON, sen. for the very valuable information communicated by him respecting the introduction of the silk-mill into Congleton and the general improvement of the town. He is also indebted to HOLLAND WATSON, ESQ, JOHN JOHNSON, ESQ. and MR. JOHN HALL, surgeon, for the several important suggestions made by them. The author also avails himself of this mode of expressing his thanks to JOHN SKERRATT, ESQ. (mayor for 1817,) and Mr. MOOREHOUSE, solicitor, the town-clerk, for their kindness in permitting him to make selections from the corporation books.

The author cannot conclude this preface in a manner more agreeable to his feelings than by cordially expressing his thanks to all the individuals who so liberally patronised his publication.

CONTENTS

The Bookselling, Bookbinding and Printing Establishment, 11 High Street, in 1896

Engraving courtesy John Condliffe

Chapter I

ANCIENT STATE

Congleton, its origin, etymology, incorporation and history till the introduction of the silk manufacture.

The origin of this pleasant, interesting and prosperous town has, like that of many great cities and towns, been left in a state of uncertainty, notwithstanding the most diligent and profound researches on the subject by learned antiquaries. From the retired situation of Congleton, at a considerable distance from the sea coast, it must, for many ages, have been a place little known and less frequented by the natives of the southern and more populous part of the island; and, notwithstanding attempts have been made to identify it with the Condate of Antoninus, it is very improbable that it ever was visited by the Romans. Hitherto there have been no remains of Roman antiquities discovered in the town or its immediate neighbourhood; nor are there any traces left to prove that the military adventurers of ancient Rome passed through the village of Congleton, in their victorious march northward.

There can be no doubt, however, that Congleton has some claim to antiquity. The natural beauty of its situation, on the banks of a pure stream, and sheltered by wood, must have pointed it out to our ancestors as a desirable place for a settlement. Accordingly, we find at the time of the general survey of England, after the conquest, Congleton contained six houses, and the population may be computed to have been about forty individuals. It is described with much apparent precision in Domesday-book[1]; and as the document must be interesting to every person connected with the town, the following is a free translation of it from the abbreviated and Monkish latin of that age[2]:— "Hugo de Mara holds Cogeltone, Godwin held it; there is one hide of land liable to pay taxes; the whole land is four carucates, of which two are occupied by two villans[3] and four borderers. There is a wood one league long and one broad; and there are two enclosed pastures. The whole is now worth four shillings."

From this authentic record it is evident that tillage was much neglected in England at, and before the time of the conquest; for although the neighbourhood of Congleton was fertile, the ground which had been cleared of wood, was merely enclosed for pasturage.

As for the etymology of the name of the town, that has never been ascertained. The probability is, that like most English towns, it is of Saxon origin, though the learned Camden in his Britannia, published in the year 1586, endeavoured to identify it with the Condate of Antoninus, as recorded in his Itinerary. As the whole passage is a curious specimen of antiquarian composition, the following translation of it from the original latin is given here.

"The Dan, or Daven, springs from the mountains which separate Cheshire from Staffordshire on the east side, and it runs without any increase to Condate[4], a town mentioned in Antoninus, and now corruptly named Congleton. Of this opinion are also Mr. Burton, Mr. Talbot and others. Wherever it was, it seems probable enough, as Mr. Burton has hinted in his comments upon the Itinerary, that it came from Condate in Gaul, famous for the death of St. Martin: for Cæsar expressly tells us that, even in his time, they translated themselves out of that part of Gaul into Britain; and that, being settled, they called their respective cities after the names of those wherein they had been born and bred. Whether any remains of Roman antiquities, that have been discovered at Congleton, induced our antiquaries to fix it there, is uncertain, since they are silent on that matter; and it is certain, that the military way, the course of the Itinerary, and the distance from Mancunium on one side and Deva on the other, all determine it to these parts; and though a Roman altar, of the inscription whereof Condati is the first word, was dug up at Conscliff, near Piercebridge, in the bishopric of Durham, yet that is wholly out of the way, and there can be no ground to remove this station thither." So much for the success of the learned Antiquarian's researches respecting Congleton; from which it is sufficiently obvious that he leaves the derivation of the name of the town in the same state of uncertainty in which he found it. But he is more circumstantial in his description of Congleton at the time he wrote, and as it was taken from an actual survey during an excursion through this part of England for the avowed purposes of collecting topographical information, his account is equally satisfactory and important, as an authentic document for the history of the town.

"The middle of this town" says he, "is watered by the little brook Howty, the east side by the Daning-Schow, and the north by the Dan. Though in consideration of its greatness, populousness, and commerce, it has deserved a mayor and six aldermen to govern it: yet it has only one chapel in it; and that entirely of wood, unless it be the choir and a little tower. The mother-church, to which it belongs, is Astbury, about two miles off, which is, indeed, a curious fabric. Such was the state of Congleton towards the close of the sixteenth century; but as Camden does not particularize the branches of commerce which contributed to the prosperity of the town, and the modern manufactures of silk and cotton, which have really enriched it, were then unknown in England, he probably means the manufacture of tag-leather-laces and gloves, and the common handicraft arts carried on in the place, for the accommodation of the inhabitants, and the farmers and villagers of the surrounding country.

Congleton, unquestionably, derived its first prosperity from the particular privileges granted by Henry de Lacy's charter to free burgesses. This charter, so important in its consequences, does not bear any date, but was certainly granted about the commencement of the fourteenth century. The noble donor of this valuable grant was of royal descent. According to Camden, William the Conqueror conferred Cheshire upon Hugh Lupus, his nephew, under the greatest and most honourable tenure that a possession was ever held by a subject; namely, to hold to him and his heirs, as freely by the sword; as the King held his crown.

An ancient manuscript, dated 1400, contains the pedigree of Hugh Lupus and his descendants, with notes illustrative of the origin of their power to grant charters. Hugh Lupus gave the barony of Halton in Cheshire, to his kinsman; Nigellus. This barony contained nine knight's fees[5], and three fourths, including the manor of Congleton; and Nigellus according to this grant enjoyed many powers and immunities, Edward the first confirmed these powers to Henry de Lacy, Earl of Lincoln, then Lord of Halton, Constable of Chester, and the eighth in descent from Nigellus. To the munificence of this nobleman the inhabitants of Congleton were indebted for their first charter; and from that period, this borough became an object of popular attention in consequence of the beneficial immunities granted to its freemen. Whatever may be the objections to the circumscribed nature of royal and noble charters, they certainly contributed in the earlier ages to the prosperity of corporate bodies, which by the enjoyment of peculiar franchises, were enabled to pursue the useful arts, manufactures, and commerce, with the utmost advantage. Congleton, indeed, from its inland situation, did not profit much by foreign traffic; but gradually increased in population, extent and opulence, by the steady industry of the inhabitants; who protected by the fortified city of Chester, from the incursions of the Welsh, and too far from London itself, to be involved in those political convulsions which occasionally shook the seat of government, kept "the noiseless tenor of their way" in comparative peace and tranquillity.

A weekly market, to be held on Saturday, in Congleton, was granted by Edward the first to Henry de Lacy, in the year 1272; and an annual fair of three days, to be held on the Festival of the Holy Trinity. This fair has long been discontinued.

According to a charter granted by Edward the first to Henry de Lacy, all the possessions conferred on him were on his demise, and that of his heirs, to become parcel of the Duchy of Lancaster, as was afterwards the case. This charter is preserved in the Duchy court of the county palatine of Lancaster, and the following is a copy.

"Edward by the Grace of God, King of England, Lord of Ireland, and Duke of Aquitaine, To all to whom these presents shall come, greeting. Know ye that our beloved and faithful Henry de Lacy of Lincoln, and constable of Chester, hath granted and quit-claimed to us for himself and his heirs, all his castles, &c. in Lancashire and Cheshire, with sundries in Yorkshire, with all the lands which Alice de Lacy, his mother, holds as her dower in the county of Lancaster, and which at her death should return to him and his heirs. To have and to hold to us and our heirs, together with knight's fees, advowsons of churches, &c. That we for his laudable service have given, granted, and by this charter have confirmed for us and our heirs, to the said Earl, all his castles, &c. aforesaid; to have and to hold to the said Earl, and the heirs of his body begotten, &c. Yet so, that if the said Earl should die without heirs of his body begotten, then upon the death of the said Earl himself, and his heirs aforesaid, all his castles, lands, &c. may remain to our dear brother, and his heirs for ever. Given under our hand at Westminster, the 28th of October, in the 22nd year of our reign, A.D. 1294." Henry de Lacy died in the year 1310, and was interred with great pomp in St. Paul's cathedral, London.

The progress of civilisation in the inland towns of England, during the early period of our foreign commerce, was slow, for even the inhabitants of our seaports derived little refinement from an intercourse with the continental nations, which were then nearly as rude as themselves. Yet Congleton, though in a remote situation, attained a decided superiority over those neighbouring towns and villages, which did not enjoy the immunities conferred by a charter.

In the fifteenth century the population of Congleton was indeed inconsiderable, and the buildings in the town of that rude kind of architecture which was general throughout England, while the arts were yet in their infancy. The best houses in the town were then built of wood and plaster, or what are commonly distinguished by the name of half-timbered houses; they were low, incommodious, and thatched with straw.

With the progressive refinement of society and increase of population, the appearance of the town also improved. Houses of brick were built by some of the opulent burgesses; the streets were widened and paved; and the inhabitants instead of solemnizing divine worship at the church of Astbury, erected a chapel of ease on the site of the present church. This edifice, the first erected in the town, is described by the accurate Camden as a structure built entirely of wood, except the choir, and tower.

The only memorable event recorded respecting Congleton during the fifteenth century, was an inundation of the river dane, which overflowed part of mill street and injured the houses and property of the inhabitants. At this period the King's mills were in a state of decay, and the burgesses of Congleton availing themselves of the accidental injury which they sustained from the inundation, petitioned Henry the sixth for permission to cut a new channel for the river, and also to remove the mills to the spot where they now stand. Their petition was granted, and the property of the mills transferred to the corporation by royal charter, dated in the year 1451.

A very important privilege was granted to the burgesses of Congleton by Henry the eighth, on the 26th of April, 1532, by which they were exempted from appearing at the courts. As this mandate is but short, and affords a specimen of the English language at that time, we shall present it for the gratification of the curious reader.

This royal injunction was equally satisfactory and beneficial to the burgesses of Congleton, as it protected them from vexatious litigation, and consequent loss of time and expense; for the officers of their own corporation were qualified by charter, to administer justice within their own jurisdiction.

In order to promote the rising prosperity of the town, it was thought expedient to confer some peculiar privilege on those freemen who were residents. A petition was consequently presented to Queen Mary in the year 1556, who granted a decree, that resident freemen only should have votes in the election of the mayor.

The accession of Elizabeth to the throne of England, was a glorious era in the history of the kingdom; and Congleton among other towns shared the benefits conferred by that wise and patriotic

HENRY the viijth by the grace of god Kyng of Englond & of France Defender of the faythe and lord of Irelond TO our trusty and Welbelovyd the Justics of Assise and to All other offics of Chestr & to evry of theym gretyng WHERas grevous compleynt ye made unto us on the behalff of our mair & coalitie of our ToWWne of Congleton parsll of our duchie of Lancastr in our Countie of Chestr HOWWE then upon playnte and other suggestyons made bifor you at Chestr agenst divrs of our sayed Inhitnnts of Congleton aforesayed Wherupon thofficers of Chestr aforesayed have distrayned theym at Congleton & in other plats WWin the libitie of our sayed duchie to apper as well at Chestr as at Countie Hyers Shirfftornes & other Courts WWin the libtie of Chestr agenst their Ancyent Charter by our Pgenitors to theym made & by us confyrmed & agenst their Ancyent Customs ther out of tyme used to their grete oppression & inquietnes of our sayed tennts & Inhitnnts of our sayed ToWWne of Congleton & in the breche of the libtyes of our sayed duchie WWe not Wyllyng their Ancyent good customs ne the libtie of our sayed duchie to be so usurped & broken Will & desir you & Natheles charge you that from hensforthe in no WWyse ye do distrayn any of our sayed tennts & Inhitnnts of our sayed ToWWne or lordshype of Congleton WWin the libtie of our sayed duchie to apper at Chestr or at any of your Countyes Hyers Hundreds Shiroffetornes or Courts for any manr of cause contrary to their sayed Chartor Franches & Ancyent Customs aforsayed Not faylyng thus to do as ye tendr our pleasur GEVEN at WWestmir under our Seal of our sayed duchye the xxvjth day of Aprell the xxiiij yer of our Reygne sovereign. From the 14th year of the reign of that illustrious Queen, the records of Congleton were preserved in the corporation books, and present a series of authentic documents illustrative of the history of the town.

Queen Elizabeth, by charter granted to the burgesses of Congleton, on the 3rd of January, 1583, ratified the charters of her predecessors, and established the privileges of the corporation upon the basis of an enlightened polity. At the first court held under that charter, on the 9th day of March, 1583, no less than two hundred individuals were sworn in freemen; a proof that the town was then populous; and from the number of officers appointed to regulate the trades and occupations of the inhabitants, considerable business was transacted here. The minutes are curious as affording a view of the progress of civilization.

"At this court five men were sworn to be viewers over all kinds of victuals.

Two sworn to be searchers and sealers of leather.

William Wyttacars, senior, currier; sworn to be dresser of tanned leather.

Three sworn to be viewers over all kinds of leathermen.

Two sworn to be viewers over all kinds of mercers, drapers, and such like.

Six sworn to be viewers over all such persons as carry fuel, called burlymen."

From this extract we may perceive that the laws of the borough had hitherto been very imperfect or negligently administered; but the corporation being now empowered by the charter of Elizabeth to enact bye laws for the regulation of this community, and to punish offenders who violated them, with a proviso that those laws should not be contrary to the statutes of the realm, a more efficient mode of government was adopted, and many excellent regulations established during the mayoralty of Richard Green, who appears to have been an active and public spirited magistrate.

At the second court of orders held by him, on the 8th day of April, 1584, it was enjoined that every householder should send his young persons to church to be instructed in the catechism. There we have an instance of the beneficial effects of the reformation. Before its benign influence operated on the human mind in this highly favoured nation, the christian religion was enveloped in mysterious gloom and secrecy by a crafty and venal priesthood, but since the establishment of the protestant church in this country, evangelical wisdom, and the refinements of science have exalted the national character to a degree of intelligence, virtue, and civilisation, unknown among any other people, or at any former period in the history of the world.

By an excellent regulation made at this period, it was ordered that the mayor should have the care of poor fatherless children, to bring them up in the fear of God, and some good trade or occupation. Another proof of the efficacious influence of that religion which enjoins the practice of charity.

That the burgesses were sufficiently tenacious of their franchises, and unwilling to admit unprivileged settlers among them is evident from a bye-law, passed on the 26th of May 1584, which enjoins that "no person shall keep any inmate, being a stranger, without licence from the mayor and court, on pain of forfeiting for every month sixteen shillings". This penalty was doubtless a sufficient prohibition; and however inhospitable such a regulation may appear, it was probably very justifiable from the peculiar circumstances of the times, as the utmost zeal and finesse were exerted by the adherents of popery, to prevent the new proselytish protestantism; and every subterfuge of bribery, menace, and anathema employed to retard the progress of truth.

It is pleasing to view the progressive improvements of a civilised community. We have already seen that proper persons were appointed to regulate the markets, and to examine, or inspect the goods offered for sale in the shops. The cleanliness, comfort, and health of the inhabitants, also became proper objects of municipal attention, and it was ordered, "that the viewers of the three wells, namely stock well, valow's well, and the well at lawton-street end, should appoint three neighbours to keep clean and sweet the said wells; and that five persons appointed for the purpose should give warning to all householders, to clean the street every Saturday evening before their houses, unto the crest or middle of the pavement"

An efficient and active police appears to have been established in Congleton, in 1584, for according to a recorded bye-law, it was ordered, "That if any man's sons, servants or apprentices, be taken by the officers, in the streets or town, after nine of the clock in the night that it shall be lawful for the officers to put such persons in the prison, there to remain during the mayor's pleasure." As this law was made on the 9th of November, it was probably intended to operate as a preventive to riot and licentiousness during the winter season.

In the year 1585, three persons were licensed to keep inns, and forty-two to keep alehouses in Congleton, on their giving bonds of forty shillings each, that they would not suffer any unlawful games to be played in their houses, nor receive stolen goods, nor harbour suspicious persons. From the number of public-houses licenced at this period, and the restrictions mentioned, there must have been a very active intercourse kept up between this and other towns; and it was then, as it still continues to be, a great thoroughfare to and from London and Lancashire.

From the most ancient institutions of society, it has ever been thought expedient to impress the public mind with respect for those who exercised legal authority, for this purpose peculiar habiliments and pompous insignia of office have been invented. The corporation of Congleton, in imitation of that of London, Chester and other privileged communities, adopted an uniform garb to be worn on particular occasions, as appears from the following order, in the town records, dated the 6th day of October, 1585. "Every person that now is of the council of this town, and is, or hath heretofore been bailiff, or catchpole, shall have at their own charges a gown, and wear the same, before the first day of May next, and also all the other persons of the council shall have of their own charges, a gown or seemly black cloak before the said first day of May. All which persons shall also wear the same, every fair day that the mayor shall walk the fairs, on pain of forfeiting twenty shillings." There appears to have been some difficulty in carrying this order into effect, for at a subsequent court held on the 27th of April, in the following year, the time for providing the gowns and cloaks was extended from the "1st of May, to the 15th of August, or feast of the assumption of the blessed Virgin Mary."

In the year 1589, during the mayoralty of Matthew Moreton, the bye-laws for the government of the borough were reviewed, most of them ratified, and new regulations enacted. The most remarkable of these were, that every freeman who should refuse to pay the fines laid on him should be disfranchised; and that no stranger be made free, nor suffered to dwell in the town or lordship, except he brought a certificate of his good behaviour, and if he had any children, he was obliged to give a bond that they should not become chargeable to the town.

Many excellent regulations had been established from the year 1582, to 1589 inclusive, for the government of the town, the prevention of disorder and vice, and the promotion of religion and morality. The education of youth was an object of too great importance to the prosperity and happiness of this community to be overlooked, and the corporation with a degree of public spirit which deserves to be recorded, instituted a grammar school, in the town in 1589, for the instruction of the sons of freemen.

The following particulars respecting the expenditure of this institution in 1590, it may not be improper to insert.

	£. s. d
"Paid to John Lowndes and others for boards for the school-house	1 0 0
To the writer his quarter's wage	0 10 0
Raufe Lowe for 20lb. candles, bell ropes, two stools and a table for the schoolmaster .	0 19 4
Mr. Tilman, schoolmaster, towards his wage	0 16 0
More in part of what is owing to him	2 15 0
Mr. Tilman, his quarter's wage, and, part of another	5 0 0
Mr. Tilman, the schoolmaster, his quarter's wage.	3 6 8
	£14 7s 0d

In 1595, the wages paid quarterly to Mr Browster, for "saying service and teaching school" was £3. 6s. 8d. or £13. 6s 8d per annum; and it is recorded, that the same year "William Hulm preached five times for five shillings," by which it appears that preaching and reading or saying the church service, were considered two distinct offices.

The liberality of the corporation was not confined to benevolent institutions, they were also generous to those occasional visitors who contributed to their amusement, or were entitled to attention for their rank and respectability. In the records for 1595, amongst other disbursements, the sum of one pound was paid to the Queen's players; three shillings and eight-pence for wine to the rush-bearers; four shillings and eight-pence for wine bestowed on Edward Fitton, esq.; and five shillings to Mr Hagerstone's man who had bears with him.

Among the sports and pastimes which the inhabitants of Congleton enjoyed in common with the rest of the people of England, were bear-baiting, and the royal sport of cockfighting. These were exhibited in the town on the 5th, 6th, and 7th of May 1601; a time of festivity mentioned in the town records as the Great Cockfight.

During this festival the sum of six shillings and eight-pence was spent in wine, cakes, and sugar, to treat Sir John Savage, the Queen's steward for the borough; an equal sum was paid to the bearward, who had the charge of the town's bear; and two shillings and sixpence for wine and sugar, for Sir John Savage and gentlemen, on the first day of the Great Cockfight.

In this age of refinement we may censure the amusements of bear-baiting and cockfighting as barbarous but they certainly had a tendency to make the different classes of society more social with each other than they now are; and to promote health and hilarity, by frequent assemblages in the open air. The ceremony of rushbearing, and strewing the floors of churches with them, originated in popish times when people were more accustomed to kneel at the public worship of the Deity than they are at present.

There is a record which demonstrates the increasing opulence of the corporation in 1590 when four members of the council were appointed to keep the keys of the town's box and be overseers of the disposal of the town's goods.

It appears that an unsuccessful attempt was made in 1601, by the Queen's bailiff, to exact more than the usual sum paid by those who brought cattle and other merchandise to the fairs and markets; for it is recorded in the corporation books, "that during the memory of man, until of late that the contrary is offered by Mr. Stubbs, her Majesty's bailiff, the toll usual paid on market days and fair days was:— For every fair day for a beast, two-pence; market day, one penny. For standing in the streets on fair days, one penny; on market days, one halfpenny. For brass, pewter, &c. wares, and every foreign basket throughout the year, one penny, called a pitching penny."

Soon after the accession of James the first first to the throne of England, an additional charter was conferred upon the burgesses of Congleton, which by the ratification of former royal grants, and the addition of new and extensive immunities has been termed the magna charta of the borough[6].

The government of the tongue has in all popular assemblies been a matter of difficulty; and it is evident from existing documents that some of the members of the corporation violated public decorum, by prurience of speech; for by a law made on the 14th of April, 1625, it was ordered "that if any alderman, capital burgess, or freeman of this borough, shall, in their public assemblies demean himself uncivilly either in speech or gesture; such offender for every such offence shall forfeit for the use of the corporation ten shillings to be levied on his goods and chattels, and for default of such payment imprisoned until he submit himself to make payment thereof."

The year 1637 was memorable in the records of Congleton, from the singular circumstance that John Bradshaw, afterwards known throughout Europe by the name of President Bradshaw, was mayor. During his mayoralty several laws were passed for the regulation of the borough, and the preservation of the inhabitants from the plague which then made dreadful ravages in Derbyshire. The strictness of the bye-law for the prevention of all intercourse with the inhabitants of infected places may appear very arbitrary, but the exigency of the case seemed to require the utmost severity of discipline. It was ordered by a decree of the mayor and common council, "that whatsoever person of this town or lordship shall presume to bring into this town any corn or fruit or other commodity, during the time of the infection in the neighbouring counties, from any such infected place, shall immediately upon his return, be shut up in his house, or some other place appointed by the mayor or justices, and shall be detained there for twenty days or longer, and to be maintained out of his own goods, if he have any, and if not, at the town's charge. And watch and ward to be kept about the said house, during the said time of restraint, as the mayor and justices shall appoint." These severe, but judicious measures of precaution appear to have averted the dreaded visitation, and the town continued to prosper till the spring of 1641, when the plague which had been brought down from London to North Rode in a box of cloth, was suddenly communicated to the circumjacent country, and soon reached Congleton. It first infected an inhabitant of the name of Laplove, whose house was immediately surrounded by wardens, who were paid one shilling each, for every twenty-four hours of this perilous employment. But all precautions against the contagion proved ineffectual, and the town soon presented a general scene of distress and dismay. In March, 1641, the plague prevailed throughout the town; a few persons made their escape on the first alarm, forsaking their property to save their lives. Of those who remained, a large proportion were soon infected. The diseased were shut up in their own houses, or in the pesthouse appropriated for their reception by the magistrates; and two-pence a day allowed from the treasury of the corporation for the support of each patient. But all communication with their friends and neighbours was prevented by the vigilance of the wardens, who were successively appointed to watch the houses where infected persons were confined, and to supply them with medicine and food.

This calamitous visitation completely dissolved all the social ties of kindred, and suspended all intercourse, not only with other parts of the kingdom, but even with a next door neighbour! For more than a year the plague spread destruction through Congleton, and the majority of its inhabitants died. Every kind of business was suspended, except that of providing the mere necessaries of life, and such medicines as were efficacious in the alleviation of pain, or the restoration of strength to the few convalescent patients, who survived this most fatal of all the diseases to which the human frame is subject.

In the course of the year 1641 Congleton became almost entirely depopulated, and so desolate that grass grew in the principal streets and nearly covered the pavement. There is no record in the corporation books of the number of persons who died; it raged in the town from the 4th of March, 1641, when several infected persons were shut up in their own houses, and in the pesthouse, till the spring of 1642, for on the 26th of May of that year, the goods and clothing of some persons recently deceased, and who were supposed to have died of the plague, were ordered by the mayor to be buried. As for the depopulation of the town, there is a proof on record how general it was; for at an Assembly holden before George Forde, mayor, June 23, 1642, it was ordered, that the said mayor should provide clean and fresh clothes for ALL the people now within the cabins, being nine in number, at the common charge of the town's box. The term "Assembly" is adopted on the occasion of this public meeting, instead of the usual terms of mayor, alderman, and common council, a demonstrative proof of the depopulated state of this once flourishing community, and the disorganization of its body corporate.

Several months elapsed before the town was considered a safe place of abode, and thoroughly purified from infection, by the destruction of clothing, bedding, and whatever was considered contagious; the return of individuals to their former habitations must consequently have been slow, if not reluctant; and little traffic could be expected with those persons who had formerly frequented the place when the inhabitants were healthful and prosperous. Yet even in this period of adversity, vice presumed to interrupt the restoration of order and propriety; but it was punished by the magistrates with a spirit and promptitude that deserves to be recorded. The following memorandum of the transaction, in the corporation books, is dated Sept 24th, 1642. "Whereas information hath been given unto the mayor, of several disorders committed by Richard Rode, of this borough, tippler, viz. that he is vehemently suspected for keeping and maintaining bawdry, and suffering divers persons of ill government to continue drinking in his house at undue hours; and that he is an enemy to the peace and welfare of this borough. Therefore the mayor and justices have thought it requisite, and do hereby under their hands suppress the said Richard Rode."

Among other persons of distinction who visited Congleton in the year 1642, William, father of the brave and unfortunate James, Earl of Derby, honoured the corporation with his presence, and was entertained by them at the expense of nine shillings and four-pence.

During the civil war between the adherents of Charles the first, and those of the parliament, the town of Congleton suffered little inconvenience or loss. Perhaps the diminished state of its population was the principal cause of the exemption. In 1645 the corporation furnished six men to the army of the parliament; they were ordered to Nantwich by summons, and were paid one shilling a day, or two-pence each. In the course of the same year, some of the sequestrators employed by parliament to levy money and confiscate the property of their enemies, came to Congleton, and demanded the sum of twenty pounds, the property of John Waller, alderman. This was paid after some delay and formality, merely resorted to for the purpose of keeping up an appearance of dignity and independence on the part of the corporation.

In the year 1649, during the mayoralty of Thomas Spencer, who appears to have been a very active magistrate, a grievance very injurious to the prosperity of many of the resident freemen of this borough was promptly and completely redressed. This can best be explained by the tenor of the order issued by the mayor, on the occasion. "Whereas divers persons, some of them inhabitants of this borough, some out-burgesses, though they inhabit not the said borough, yet have rent coming to their purses yearly, for lands in the said borough; which said burgesses are behind and unpaid all or most of their several laies and taxations, which have been imposed on them for four years last past, whereby the well affected and willing persons of the borough have been over pressed and hurt to pay their several laies and assessments oftener than they should have done, and those persons that have been backward in their payments, have hitherto withheld their several payments contrary to the several warrants, which have come to the constable's hands for the levying thereof, and contrary to all equity and good conscience. It is therefore ordered by the mayor and common counsell, that the constables of the present year, together with all such as have been constables for four years last past, shall all of them join together, and compel payment of whatever arrears of laies are behind, for the space and time aforesaid, and by what persons, the same laies and assessments to collect and gather in by distress or otherwise, between this (August 24th,) and the 5th day of September next; at which time they are required, to give account of their doing herein to the mayor, aldermen, and common counsell of this town. And for their pains herein it is ordered, that they shall have and receive three-pence in the pound for all said monies they shall so collect. And it is further ordered, that the said constables shall for their several years, give in their several accounts of arrears respectively, to the mayor within three days after the sight of this present order."

At this period, England was under the control of Oliver Cromwell, and President Bradshaw who was chief judge at the trial of Charles the first, was high steward of Congleton. This curious fact is ascertained by a record in the corporation books, in the following words:

"Jan 21st, 1655-6. Thomas Spencer, mayor, ordered, that John Bradshaw, esq., of this borough, learned in the law, be continued high-steward of, and counsellor for this borough as formerly, and be paid the same salary quarterly, as heretofore hath been paid, and that he be acquainted therewith and his acceptance desired."

From a subsequent record, however, it appears that President Bradshaw declined the honour intend him by his brother burgesses; for it is ordered under the date, of the 19th of May following, "That a tender shall be made to the Lord Savage, of the high-stewardship of this borough, by the next post, Mr. Attorney Bradshaw having given up his interest therein." There seems something of a lurking resentment in this passage; and the corporation seem to have felt hurt at what they probably considered neglect on the part of their former townsmen. But Mr. Attorney Bradshaw was chief justice of Chester, and representative in parliament for Cheshire; it could not, therefore, be reasonably expected, that he could, however willing, devote much of his attention to the affairs of Congleton.

In the list of freemen admitted and sworn on the 23rd day of January, 1658[7], the name of "Henry Bradshaw of Marple, esq." the elder brother of President Bradshaw, is included.

The corporation seem to have been sufficiently vigilant in their prevention of encroachments upon their property, for an order appears under the date of July 16th, 1658, prohibiting any person from building a cottage upon the commons belonging to the borough; yet a liberal disposition was manifested to facilitate the intercourse between the inhabitants of Congleton and those of the neighbouring township of Buglawton, to whom five pounds were voted by the corporation, on condition that they would make a horse-bridge over Daneinshaw ford.

Soon after the restoration of Charles the second, that sovereign granted an exemplification of the former charters, to the burgesses; yet it does not appear that the new government was satisfied with the conduct of some of the members of the corporation, during the Protectorate, for on the 9th day of September, 1662, the commissioners appointed for the regulation of corporations removed four aldermen and seven capital burgesses, and appointed others in their stead. According to a new regulation it was ordered that neither the present mayor nor justices, nor any other alderman should serve as mayor or justice before it came to their turn successively.

On the 9th day of October, 1662, Matthew Lowndes was sworn jail keeper, and a list delivered, to him particularizing the bolts, locks, and manacles belonging to the prison; a bridle for scolding women, and the mace.

The year 1667, was memorable in the records of Congleton, for a charter granted to the burgesses by Charles the second. This royal grant, however, was nothing more than a ratification of the charters conferred by former sovereigns.

An idea may be conceived of the very unsettled state of the church, and the general laxity of public morals about the time of the restoration, from the curious fact, that it was with difficulty the corporation could obtain the attendance of a minister weekly, at the chapel of this town. At a meeting of the mayor, aldermen, and common council, October 15th, 1661, it was agreed, "that every one of the counsell do endeavour to procure a minister, to supply this place for one sabbath-day apiece, until such time as an able minister shall be agreed upon by this counsell, to be hired to be constant minister within this borough; and that, in the mean time there be ten shillings a sabbath, paid out of the stock unto such minister. And that the mayor do provide for the first sabbath; and so every one else in their several turns."

In the year 1669, a Mr. Barber, then minister of the corporation chapel, had an offer made to him of the superintendence of the free-school established in the borough; but he seems to have been ungrateful to the burgesses, and even negligent of his duties, in consequence of which he was silenced by the authority of the mayor and common council, in the following curious mandate which, although not remarkable for correctness of composition, is sufficiently intelligible, and perfectly significant of the dismissal of the refractory priest, "March 17th, 1669. Being that Mr. Barber, minister, hath neglected and slited the whole town very much, it is this day ordered, that he shall not preach any more in our chappel" Down to this period the corporation appear to have exercised unlimited authority, in the appointment, or suspension of their clergy; but, soon afterwards when the church was more firmly established, the bishop of the diocese very properly examined the minister nominated by the corporation and authorized him to preach. On the 19th of May, 1674, it was ordered by the mayor and common council, "that Mr. Harrison be hired to be minister of the chapel of this borough for one half year, provided he be allowed of by the bishop of this diocese, to exercise the said function." Much irregularity had doubtless occurred during the civil wars, in the solemnization of the rites of the church; and when Cromwell assumed sovereign powers with the title of Lord Protector, the utmost extravagance of fanaticism pervaded the state; but after the restoration, the episcopacy resumed legal functions and notwithstanding the licentiousness of the court, a superior degree of public decency, and genuine religious feeling gradually prevailed throughout England.

According to the records preserved in the corporation books, the freedom of this borough, was purchasable; and from the price demanded for admission to these franchises, the rising prosperity of the town may be ascertained. In 1669, Susannah Walker paid five pounds for her freedom; in April, 1681, Joseph Gray was admitted a freeman on paying ten pounds; and on the 18th of November following, Nathaniel Bateman was admitted to exercise his trade in this borough and to be a freeman thereof, paying to the corporation the sum of fourteen pounds. It is observable that females were admitted to the privileges of the borough, and the following curious proviso was recorded respecting the admission of Susannah Walker above mentioned. "If in case she chance to marry, her husband is to be free of any trade in this borough, for the aforesaid five pounds, already paid in the presence of John Walker, mayor, &c."

On the accession of James the second, many congratulatory addresses were presented to his Majesty from the inhabitants of different cities and towns. The burgesses of Congleton also offered their felicitations on this occasion, as appears by a record dated May 4th, 1684, when it was ordered by the mayor &c. "That an address to his sacred Majesty King James the second, be drawn up and presented to congratulate his Majesty's peaceable and happy entrance on his reign and government; whom God save, and send him long to reign. Amen."

During the reign of William and Mary, this town in common with every other part of the British empire, experienced the beneficial influence of good government, and the gradual extension of foreign commerce, and domestic traffic; but it was not yet distinguished for any particular manufacture, except that of tag-leather-laces, called " Congleton points."

In the year 1698, two members of the corporation were disfranchised on account, of their poverty; and in 1701, an alderman of this borough was expelled, for absenting himself from his public duty, and being a common drunkard, a common swearer, and committing other misdemeanours.

Many residents who were not freemen had from time to time been fined for carrying on their respective trades in this borough, and an order was issued by the mayor, in 1709, by which thirty-two persons, were required to pay a certain sum per quarter. But in most instances the person fined was previously invited to become a burgess.

The corporation with commendable zeal for religion, and the improvement of public morals in their community, had for ages paid the salaries of the minister of their chapel, and the master of their free-school, out of the funds of the borough. In June, 1709, Mr. Malbon, the minister was elected head master with a salary of one pound per quarter, and what he could make by country scholars and perquisites; and Thomas Bourne was elected under master, with a salary of three pounds per quarter; on condition that he gave a bond of £100, to resign at half a year's notice, if required, by the major part of the corporation. Mr. Bourne appears to have performed his duty as the instructor of the freemen's sons entirely to the satisfaction of the corporation, for on the 13th of January, 1719 it was ordered, "that Mr. Thomas Bourne be made a freeman gratis, he having been the under schoolmaster several years, and having discharged his trust to the corporation, like an honest, painful ingenious, careful gentleman." The school was certainly highly beneficial to the youth of the town and its vicinity; it had been enlarged by an additional room fourteen feet square, erected in the garden belonging to it, in the year 1714; and derived considerable popularity as well as importance from the abilities and application of the two active and meritorious teachers, employed at this period.

It appears that the emolument attached to the office of chief magistrate of Congleton was very inconsiderable a century ago; for on the 3rd of October, 1725, it was ordered, "That the mayor in future shall have the tolls of shrovetide fair, as a perquisite, towards carrying off the said office of mayor decently." By another order dated May 16th, 1726, it appears that the principal law officer of the corporation, was paid a very small salary; for it was ordered, "that Thomas Bowyer, esq. shall for the future be employed as counsellor for this borough; and that he shall have forty shillings paid out of the town's box.'

Few communities have so happily escaped the antisocial influence of party spirit as that of Congleton; yet, even here discord has in a few instances interrupted the general harmony. In the reign of Queen Anne, the burgesses of this town in common with the rest of their country-men, were divided into two parties, denominated whig and tory; the former of which were the advocates for the constitutional liberties of the people, and the restriction of the aristocracy and monarchy; the latter stood forth the champions of the hierarchy, and the royal prerogatives. On the demise of the

Queen, in the year 1714, George the first was proclaimed, but the tories would not allow the church bells to be rung. The whigs, many of whom were dissenters, on the other hand, rejoiced at the event, and hastened to the church to ring the bells. Some waggish or mischievous person had secretly tied the fire-bell to one of the other bells, consequently when the merry peal was raised the alarm bell rang also, which occasioned a tumultuous assemblage of the townsmen. On the crowd rushing to the church they found some of the dissenters busily engaged, on which the tories buffeted them out of the steeple, and having collected in a large body, they proceeded to the meeting-house, near the end of mill-street, where, though the dissenters made some defence, their opponents finally prevailed; entered the place, which they completely ransacked, carrying away the pulpit and forms to dane bridge, where they were destroyed by fire. Since that event, no instance of outrage, for mere difference of opinion, has occurred in this town.

From the frequency with which toll had been exacted from the freemen of Congleton, who frequented the markets and fairs of Macclesfield, and in direct violation of the charter granted by Henry de Lacy; the mayor of the latter town was written to on the subject, by the town-clerk, in 1729; and in consequence of this application, an agreement was reciprocally entered into by the two corporations, for the amicable prevention of future disputes, and the conservation of the peculiar privileges of the freemen of both towns, in their intercourse with each other.

During the Scotch rebellion, in the year 1745, Congleton was entered by a detachment of the rebel army, about 1,300 strong, commanded by Lord George Murray. They marched into this town on the — of December, and compelled the mayor, in all his formalities, to proclaim their Prince at the market-cross. They remained all night, and early the next morning marched away to rejoin the main body at Leek. During their short stay they searched for, and seized whatever arms they could find, lived gratuitously with respect to food and lodging, but did no injury to any person. Some of their followers, however, were guilty of several acts of plunder in the town. Part of the royal army soon afterwards passed through in pursuit of the rebels, and the decisive battle of Culloden, fought on the 16th of April following, completely quelled the rebellion.

To this time, the progress of Congleton in opulence and refinement, was gradual and slow; but a more auspicious and prosperous era approached, when the genius and enterprize of commercial adventure successfully established a lucrative branch of an elegant manufacture here.

REFERENCES

1. To some of our readers it may be necessary to offer a brief account of this very valuable and ancient record: this we shall do in the words of Ingulphus, who was Secretary to William the Conqueror, by whose order the survey of Domesday was made: "King William for the taxing of his whole land, tooke this order in all England, there was not an hide of land but he knew the value thereof and the possessor also, neither meire nor place there was, but it was valued in the King's role, the rents and profits, the possession and possessor, were made manifest and knowne unto the King, according to the fidelitie of taxors, which being chosen out of every countrey taxed or seized their own territories or made their own rent role. This role is called the role of Winton, and of the Englishmen for the generaltie thereof, containing wholie all the tenements of ye whole land, it is named Domesday. Such a role and very like did King Alfred once set forth, in which he taxed all the lande of Englande by Shires, Hundreds and "Tythings".

2 "Isdem Bigot tenet Cogeltone Godvinus tenuit; ibi una hida geldabilis: terra est IV carucarum; ibi sunt II cum II villanis et IV bordariis. Silva ibi una leuua longa, et una lata; et ibi II haiæ. Wasta fuit, et sic invenitur; moda valet IV solidos."

3. Villan or villein is another name for slave. They were formerly attached either to the lands or to the person of the landholder; and transferrable like cattle. In the former case they were called called villeins regardant, in the latter villeins in gross. Their state was gradually meliorated, though not abolished, till 1660 in the reign of Charles II. Black.Com.

4. Horsley, Baxter, and Stukely, contend, that it was at or near Northwich; Camden and Salmon fix it at Congleton; and Reynolds states that he expects Middlewich "will be found to be the very place." But the indefatigable researches of Mr. Whitaker appear decisive in establishing this disputed point; accordiug to his investigation Kinderton, near Middlewich, must have been the Condate of the Romans.

See Whitaker's Hist. of Manchester, vol. I. page 153, &c.8VO. ed.

5. William the Conqueror divided the kingdom into a certain number of Knight's Fees. The measure of each, in the reign of Edward I was estimated at twelve plough lands, or as much as could reasonably have been cultivated in a year, with twelve ploughs. The value of the Knight's Fee, which varied, was in the reign of Edward I and II stated at twenty pounds per annum. It may now be reckoned worth four hundred pounds. The pledge of personal service to the king for the Knight's Fee, degenerated into a pecuniary commutation, and was finally abolished in the twelfth year of Charles II. Black. Com.

6. See Charters, &c. Chapter VI.

7. See Appendix.

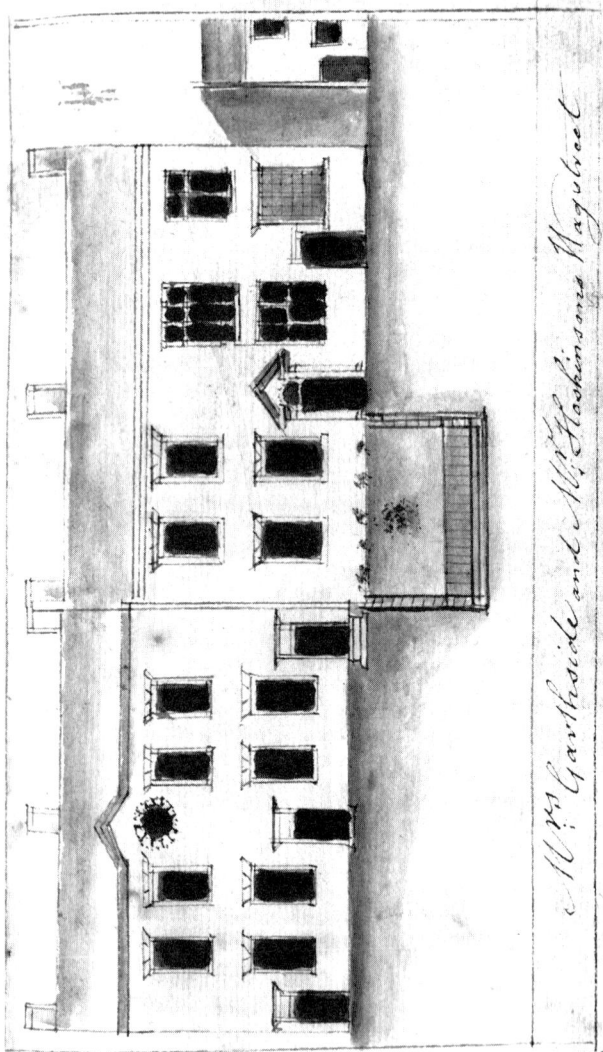

Mr. Garthside and Mr. Hodgkinsons Warehouse

CHAPTER II.
MODERN STATE.

Description, Situation, &c. – Market, – Fairs, – Manor, –
Population, – Flagging and Lighting.

Few inland towns of England present such a variety of pleasing objects to the stranger, as Congleton. The natural situation of the town itself is fine, and the scenery in its vicinity truly picturesque. The entrance by the great London road, from the west, is by a gradual and almost imperceptible descent. Near the entrance of west-street, on the left, West-house, the seat of N.M. Pattison, esq., appears, amid an enclosure skirted with a beautiful shrubbery. The house itself is a neat modern mansion of brick; one of the fronts commands a view of the subjacent valley, and fertile fields which gradually decline to the southern bank of the Dane; and from the moderate elevation of the building, and its airy situation in a dry soil, few places of residence are more eligible. The houses on the right of west-street are small and inconsiderable near the entrance, but a little farther on the left, Mortlake-house, the residence of John Johnson, esq., banker, situated at a convenient distance from the road, amid pleasure grounds, presents an attractive object to the eye. It is a handsome modern structure of brick. Another mansion, the residence of Joseph Roe, esq., and an elegant building, the residence of William Lowndes esq., are the other most conspicuous houses on this side of the road. From the rear of all these seats, there is a richly varied prospect of the fields, meadows, and plantations, which decline gradually to the verge of the Dane, and of several silk manufactures on its banks; and the fields, houses, and wood, on the lofty hill which bounds the northern prospect. The most conspicuous object on this high ground is Hulmwalfield, the mansion of Lady Warburton. West-street is also adorned by the commodious houses of Mrs. Antrobus, and Holland Watson, esq.; and the street is terminated by the lion and swan inn, an ancient half-timbered house. On the opposite side, the coach office, and bank, terminate the northern row of houses, and the whole of west-street is about half a mile in extent.

On the right of this street is wagg-street, which contains only a few houses, but is remarkable for that neat modern edifice, the methodist chapel. On the left of west-street, the great London road, which passes through west-street, is continued through mill-street, and over Dane bridge, at its northern end. This is an irregular street, the most remarkable buildings in which are the calvinist chapel, the unitarian chapel. the post-office, and bull's head inn. Opposite this inn, a short and narrow street leads into bridge-street, on the right is the town well, over which a pump was erected in the year 1814.

There is a moderate descent into bridge-street, and thence, by a gradual ascent, the stranger advances into high-street, and the market-place. This is the most ancient part of the town; but many of the houses have been rebuilt in the present age; consequently, the appearance is not uniform, but extremely irregular; for several of the old buildings that remain are half-timbered houses, which have a comparatively mean appearance, contrasted with the more commodious and modern dwellings of brick. The market-place is a wide street, sufficiently spacious for the purposes of buying and selling provisions. Rows of booths and stalls are erected in it on the market-day, on each side, with an intermediate space sufficiently wide for the passage of waggons, and other carriages. Several handsome shops in the market-place and high-street, present a pleasing variety of objects to the passenger's eye. These streets also contain some good inns, particularly the roe-buck and golden lion. The market-place is terminated on the left by the town-hall, a modern edifice adorned with a neat piazza.

From the market-place, the stranger descends into a short street, which leads by a considerable ascent into lawton-street, chiefly remarkable for an ancient mansion, said to have been the residence of President Bradshaw. Lawton-street terminates the extent of the town to the east.

Opposite the town-hall, chapel-street extends irregularly

southward. It contains several good buildings and the parsonage-house, the dwelling of the reverend Samuel Williamson. The church and church-yard are situated on a moderate elevation a little to the left of chapel-street. At the termination of this street, moody-street appears on the right. It is a short street, situated on the southern declivity of a gentle eminence which gradually declines into the market-place. Moody-street contains some well-built houses, of which Moody-house, and Moody-hall, are the most extensive and conspicuous. Southward of moody-street, two modern silk manufactures terminate the buildings in a very pleasing manner, as they afford a demonstration of the commercial prosperity and spirit of improvement which prevails in this town.

The rapid current of the river Dane formerly washed the northern verge of Congleton, flowing in a semilunar direction till it reached the end of mill-street, but as the town was liable to injury from the sudden inundations of that river, when swollen into a flood, by the streams from the Cheshire and Staffordshire hills near its source, the current was turned into a new channel, which extended close to the east of the northern woody hill, in the deepest part of the valley, thus leaving a considerable flat space of fertile and luxuriant meadow and pasturage between the river and the town. Mr. Ormerod, in his history of Cheshire, has erroneously described Congleton, as "delightfully situated in a deep valley on the banks of the Dane." The real situation of the town is on a gentle and gradual eminence rising from the meadows on the southern banks of the dane, and terminated on the south by the high ground at the extremity of moody-street, and chapel-street. Two small vallies intersect Congleton at equal distances, through which two inconsiderable rivulets flow, one of which, the Howty, has sometimes inundated part of the town, after a heavy fall of rain on the southern hills in the vicinity. The principal part of the town is built on a sandy soil, and it is well supplied with excellent spring water. Although Congleton has suffered by the occasional visitation of the plague and other epidemical diseases, yet the air is wholesome, and numerous instances of longevity have occurred among the inhabitants.

The appearance of the surrounding country is beautiful, gradually rising into picturesque hills and sinking into fertile vallies, especially on the Cheshire side. The highest hills are the barren ridges of the Mole-cop and Cloud, which form the back ground of the scene, at the distance of four miles eastward, constituting part of the Staffordshire Morelands. Such is the general outline of the topography of Congleton.

The antiquity of Congleton as a borough, has been clearly ascertained and already mentioned, but it does not appear from any records extant, that its burgesses ever possessed the elective franchise; consequently, they never returned any representatives in parliament.

With respect to its collateral and geographical situation, Congleton is in the parish of Astbury, the hundred of Northwich, and the diocese of Chester. It is distant 161 miles from London, by the direct turnpike road through Lichfield; 55 miles from Birmingham, 43 from Liverpool, 24 from Manchester, 31 from Chester, 18 from Nantwich, 16 from Northwich, 11 from Middlewich, 14 from Knutsford, 8 from Macclesfield, 7 from Sandbach, 12 from Newcastle, 10 from Leek, and 15 from Buxton.

The market, which was granted by Edward the first to Henry de Lacy, is held on Saturday, when there is an abundant supply of butcher's meat, and other provisions, offered for sale. There are four fairs held annually; namely, on the Thursday before shrovetide, the 12th of May, the 10th of July, and the 22nd of November. These fairs are principally for the sale of horses, cattle, and Yorkshire woollen cloths, together with cutlery, haberdashery, and toys.

The manor of Congleton has passed into the possession of different families. According to the most ancient record extant on the subject, it was granted by Charles the first, in fee-farm to Ditchford and others[1]; some years afterwards it seems to have been in a family of the name of Toxteth[2], and to have passed by successive heiresses to the Grahams and Rawdons. In the year 1745, it was purchased from Sir John Rawdon and Helena his wife, by Peter Shakerley, esq.; and has since devolved to C.W.J. Shakerley, esq. of Somerford Park, who had an allotment as lord of the manor, when the commons were enclosed under the authority of an act of Parliament, passed in 1795.

At the second enumeration of the population of Great Britain, by the order of an act of Parliament in 1811, Congleton contained 944 inhabited houses, 30 uninhabited, and 5 building. The number of families was 986, of whom 158 were employed in agriculture; 750 in trade, manufactures, or handicraft; and 78 not comprized in the two preceding classes. The number of males was 2,028; females 2,593; total 4,616. Since that time there has been a regular increase in this, as well as most other towns and the present population may be estimated at 5000 persons, or upwards.

A truly praiseworthy attention to the welfare of their little community seems ever to have actuated the corporation, of this fact, numerous records in the books afford a complete illustration. Taverns and alehouses have been but too often proved time nurseries of vice, and introduced habits of drunkenness, idleness, and gambling, with their usual train of dreadful consequences. A vigilant magistracy will, therefore, endeavour to prevent the evils of licentiousness by judicious restrictions, and by diminishing the number of these receptacles for the idle and profligate, of this, there is an instance under the date of July 29th, 1763, during the mayoralty of Joseph Hill, when it was ordered, that not above thirty-four alehouses should be licensed for the borough; a number which was by no means too great, when the circumstance of an increasing population in a town that was the great thoroughfare between London, Liverpool, and Manchester, is considered.

On the 4th of February, 1803, the sum of £200 was ordered by the corporation towards altering the turnpike road, or principal thoroughfare through mill-street. This liberal grant was, doubtless, made to facilitate the general advantages attainable by the improved state of the turnpike road from London to Manchester and Liverpool, which passes through west street and mill-street. In 1784, the old bridge over the Dane, which was both narrow and in a decayed state, was pulled down, and rebuilt on a much larger scale at the expense of seven hundred pounds. The old bridge was only about three yards wide, and of a considerable length, composed of six arches, some of which were semi-circular and some elliptical; part of these had been carried away by floods and the rapid current of the Dane, and the bridge had been repaired from time to time in a very clumsy and imperfect manner. When taken down it consisted of one large arch, and four small. The new bridge is a handsome and substantial piece of masonry, eight yards wide, and fifty four yards long, supported by three large and strong arches.

Among other memorable events must be mentioned a royal visit to this ancient borough. On the 6th of November, 1806, his Royal Highness the Prince of Wales passed through Congleton, where he was received with all possible deference by the mayor, aldermen, common council, and most of the inhabitants. On this occasion the following address was delivered to the illustrious visitor. "May it please your Royal Highness, We his Majesty's, your Royal Father's loyal subjects, the mayor, aldermen, burgesses, and high steward, of the borough of Congleton, humbly approach your Royal Highness with our most respectful congratulations on your entrance into our most gracious Sovereign's county palatinate of Chester, of which ancient city your Royal Highness is earl; we devoutly pray that when it shall please God to finish the glorious course of his most sacred and illustrious Majesty, your Royal Highness may be a blessing to and long reign over, a free, prosperous, and happy people. We felicitate ourselves on the fortunate occasion which enables us to express those feelings of respect and affection which we must ever entertain towards your Royal Highness and every part of your august family."

To this congratulatory address, the Prince returned the following most gracious answer[3].

"To the mayor, aldermen; burgesses, and high steward of the borough of Congleton. - The universal sentiments of attachment and regard which have been manifested towards my person in every part of the country through which I have passed, and so conspicuous in your ancient borough, have filled me with emotions not to be erased. Your welcome, particularly, on my entrance into the county palatine from which I derive one of my proudest honors, affords me additional gratification. And I desire to assure you that the dearest wish of my heart must and ever shall be to promote the welfare and happiness of these kingdoms."

On the 13th day of October, 1817, the boundaries of the township were perambulated by the mayor, John Johnson, esq., and the other members of the corporation, in their appropriate robes of office, accompanied by C.W.J. Shakerley, esq., lord of the manor, and a multitude of people who were attracted by the novelty of the spectacle. This ceremony was rendered more gratifying, and the scene more enlivening, by an unclouded sky throughout the day. The procession set out from the town-hall, at nine o'clock in the morning, and returned at six in the the evening. Near a century had elapsed since the former perambulation of the boundaries of this ancient borough.

Among the modern improvements, the inhabitants, in 1814, lighted their streets, and the householders partially flagged the causeways opposite their abode. West-street was flagged at the expense of Sir Edmund Antrobus bart. whose liberal benefactions in support of the different public institutions and improvements of the town, entitled him to, and have secured the gratitude and esteem of the residents.

REFERENCES
1. Record in the Duchy of Lancaster-office.
2. Lyson's Magna Britannia
3. Spoken by himself in substance, and afterwards presented in writing to John Johnson, esq. the then mayor.

CHAPTER III.
CIVIC GOVERNMENT OF THE BOROUGH.

The Corporation, – Sessions, – Courts Leet, –
List of Subordinate Officers, – Salaries, –
Lists of Mayors, and High Stewards and their Deputies,
from 1584 to 1819, – Guild-Hall, Workhouse.

The corporation, first instituted by the charter of Henry Lacy, and afterwards favoured with an extension of their franchises by Royal grants and charters of successive sovereigns, now consists of a mayor, eight aldermen, and sixteen capital burgesses. Two of the aldermen are annually appointed justices, and are commissioned to act within the jurisdiction of the borough, and hold a general sessions of the peace in conjunction with the mayor, for the trial of misdemeanors, and also of felonies, not affecting the life or limb of the felon. Accordingly, four quarter sessions are held in the year; and also two courts leet: one in July, and the other at Martinmas, the first of which is called the mayor's court. At the latter court the constables for the following year are chosen, and the inhabitants of the borough are required to do suit and service at both these courts, and in default of their appearing to the court incur a fine, which is usually one shilling. A court is also held within the borough, called the court of pleas which has jurisdiction in civil cases to an unlimited amount, whereby, all debts contracted within the borough, may be recovered at a very trifling expense, and at which court the high steward or his deputy presides.

The court leet for this borough was formerly held here by the bailiff of the baron of Halton, but is now held before the high steward, or his deputy. By the charter of James the first, Thomas Savage, knight and baronet, was appointed the first high steward for life, and his son John Savage, knight, the second steward: after their deaths, the mayor, aldermen, and burgesses, were to appoint the future ones. The present high steward is Randle Wilbraham, esq. of Rode; and Mr. John Lockett, Solicitor, his deputy.

The mayor and town-clerk have a power (not now used) of taking recognizances of debts, and issuing executions thereon, according to the form of the statute merchant, called the statute of Acton Burnel[1]; and also, by a grant of Edward the first, to hold a court of pie-powder[2].

The present mode of electing the members of the corporate body is as follows:— The new mayor is elected by the mayor, aldermen, capital burgesses, and freemen. One of the justices (by courtesy) is nominated by the mayor elect, and the other by the mayor, aldermen, and capital burgesses, by whom the corporate vacancies are filled up, and the subordinate officers are chosen —

the latter are sworn into their offices before the mayor, who is sometimes attended by one or both of the justices. The catchpole and aletaster are chosen by the burgesses at large, at the leet, and the four constables by the court leet jury.

The serjeant at mace, who is called the mayor's serjeant, is also the jailer, and is nominated by the mayor, for the time being.

The following is a list of the petty officers, of the corporation.

Sealers of leather.	Inmate-lookers.
Scavengers.	Swine-catchers.
Market-lookers.	Chimney-lookers.
Sealers of weights and measures.	Burley-men.
Tender of the town wood	Jail-keeper.
Inspector of raw hides.	

Some of the improvements which have been made in the town, under the direction and at the expense of the corporation, are given under their respective heads. The paving of the streets, cleansing and repairing of the public sewers and wells, and the following salaries and other sums are also paid by the corporation.

	£.	s.	d.
To sundry charities	16	0	6
Schoolmaster's salary	16	0	0
Towards the minister's income	25	0	0
To the Clerk	5	5	0
Ringers' salary	8	0	0
Church sweeper's ditto	1	12	0
Deputy recorder's ditto	5	5	0
Town-clerk's ditto	2	13	4
Town-hall keeper's ditto	1	10	0
Carried forward	81	5	10
Brought forward	81	5	10
Goal-keeper's ditto, and other expenses attending the jail, averaged at	15	0	0
Dog-whipper's salary	1	6	0
Mace-bearer's ditto	10	10	0
	£108	1	10

List of the present members of the corporation.

Mayor.

NATHANIEL MAXEY PATTISON

Aldermen.

JAMES TWEMLOW,

GEORGE READE,

SAMUEL WILLIAMSON,

JOHN JOHNSON,

JONATHAN BROADHURST,

HOLLAND WATSON,

THOMAS BOWERS,

JOHN SKERRATT.

Capital burgesses.

PHILIP HALL,	J. M. WOOLFENDEN,
WILLIAM BULL,	CHARLES LOW,
THOMAS CHADDOCK,	GEORGE WILKINSON,
JOHN JACKSON,	JAMES WASHINGTON.
RICHARD LOW,	WILLIAM PEDLEY,
FRANCIS BOSTOCK,	CHARLES PEDLEY,
JESSE DRAKEFORD,	JOHN HALL,
JOHN BROADHURST,	WILLIAM CHAS. COX,

Town-clerk.

CHRISTOPHER MOORHOUSE.

List of mayors from the year 1554 to the present year 1819 — a period of 265 years;—

1554, James Rode.

1555, The same.

1556, The same.

1557, Richard Greene.

1558, The same.

1559, William Rode.

1560, Roger Greene,

1561, Richard Spencer.

1562, William Thorley.

1563, Roger Greene.

1564, The same.

1565, Richard Spencer,

1566, John Hobson.

1567, Thomas Comberbach.

1568 Roger Greene.

1569, Randell Hankinson.

1570, William Thorley.

1571, Alexander Latham.

1572, Roger Greene.

1573, The same.

1574, John Hobson.

1575, Randell Hankinson.

1576, Thos. Comberbach,

1577, Roger Greene.

1578, Alexander Latham.

1579, John Scragg.

1580, Richard Spencer.

1581, The same.

1583, John Smythe.

1584, Roger Greene.

1585, Richard Spencer.

1586, The same.

1587, Richard Green.

1588, John Hobson.

1589, Matthew Moreton.

1590, John Woulfe.

1591, Hugh Green.

1592, William Drakeford.

1593, The same.

1594, William Stubbs.

1595, Richard Spencer.

1596, — Creswell.

1597, Richard Green.

1598, John Hobson.

1599, Matthew Moreton.

1600, John Hobson.

1601, Richard Spencer.

1602, John Hobson.

1603, The same.

1604, Edward Drakeford.

1605, John Smyth.

1606, Wanting.

1607, Randle Rode.

1608 Edward Drakeford.

1609, John Latham.

1610, William Drakeford.

1611, The same.

1612, Richard Green.

1613, Henry Haworth.

1614, The same.

1615, John Hobson.

1616, Thomas Brooke.

1617, Matthew Holliday.

1618, Edward Drakeford.

1620, Thomas Parnell.

1621, Randle Rode.

1622 Roger Poynton.

1623, William Newton.

1624, Thomas Parnell.

1625, Philip Oldfield.

1626, William Knight.

1627, Richard Green.

1628, The same.

1629, John Latham.

1632, Roger Hobson.

1633, Thomas Rode.

1634, John Walker.

1635, Randle Rode.

1636, William Newton.

1637, John Bradshaw.

1638, Edward Drakeford.

1639, William Knight.

1640, John Walker.

1641, George Ford.

1642, Joseph Henshaw.

1644, John Latham.

1645, Thomas Spencer.

1646, Robert Knight.

1649, Thomas Spencer.

1655, John Latham.

1656, Robert Knight.

1657, The same.

1658, Richard Parnell.

1659, John Holliday.

1660, John Hobson

1661, Thomas Walker.

1662, Thos. Higginbotham.

1663, William Moreton

1664, Joseph Kent

1665, Ralph Hammersley.

1666, John Latham

1667, Richard Hall.

1668, John Walker.

1669, William Knight.

1670, R. Cotton.

1671, William Newton.

1672, William Harding.

1673, Robert Hobson.

1674, — Lingard.

1675, Thomas Spencer.

1676, Thomas Butcher.

1677, John Walker.

1678, — Smith.

l679, Ralph Hall.

1680, — Newton.

1681, William Harding.

1682, William Hobson.

1683, — Knight.

1684, Peter Lingard.

1685, Thomas Malbon.

1686, William Spencer.

1687, Thomas Woolwich.

1688, — Smith.

1690, William Newton.

1691, John Shaw.

1692, Robert Knight.

1693, Thomas Malbon.

1694. The same.

1695, John Shaw.

1696, Thomas Woolrich.

1698, John Vardon.

1701, John Markland.

1702, The same.

1703, William Bayley.

1704, Thomas Becket.

1705, Thomas Woolrich.

1706, William Ferne.

1707, Thomas Malbon.

1708, Thomas Malbon.

1709, John Shaw.

1710, Thomas Woolrich.

1711, William Ferne.

1712, John Vardon

1713, The same.

1714, John Toft.

1715, Thomas Shaw.

1716, John Jackson.

1717, William Gorst.

1718, Thomas Woolrich.

1719, The same.

1720, Joseph Malbon

172l, The same.

1722, William Emery.

1723, John Vardon, jun.

1724, Thomas Shaw.

1725, John Barlow.

1726, John Bostock.

1727, Samuel Brooke.

1728, Thomas Kelsall.

1729, William Emery.

1730, Thomas Bowyer.

1731, John Vardon.

1732, The same.

1733, John Bostock.

1734, Richard Thorp.

1735, John Barlowe.

1736, Richard Martin.

1737 John Smith.

1738, John Bostock.

1739, John Vardon.

1740, William Bayley.

1741, Richard Thorp.

1742, Richard Martin.

1743, Richard Thorp.

1744, John Smith.

1745, William Poynton.

1746, John Vardon.

1747, The same.

1748, John Bostock.

1749, John Drake.

1750, Richard Martin.

1751, Richard Thorp.

1752, Joseph Bramshall.

1753, Joseph Drake.

1754, John Clayton.

1755, The same.

1756, William Bayley.

1757, Joseph Bramshall.

1758, Richard Martin.

1759, The same.

1760, John Drake.

1761, The same.

1762, Joseph Hill.

1763, The same.

1764, Philip Antrobus.

1765, William Bayley.

1766, John Drake,

1767, Joseph Hill.

1768, Thomas Yearsley.

1769, Thomas Brooks.

1770, James Vardon.

1771, Richard Webster.

1772, Philip Antrobus.

1773, William Ward.

1774, Joseph Hill.

1775, The same.

1776, Thomas Yearsley.

1777, B. Leftwych Wynn.

1778, Thomas Brooks.

1779, William Reade.

1780, Philip Antrobus.

1781, John Whitfield.

1782, Thomas Yearsley.

1783, The same.

l784, Thomas Brooks.

1785, William Reader

1786, Nathaniel Maxey Pattison.

1787, Bowyer Leftwych Wynn,

1788, Richard Martin.

1789, Robert Hodgson.

1790, James Twemlow.

1791, George Reade.

1792, Thomas Garside.

1793. John Shaw Reade.

1794, John Dean.

1795, Joseph Vardon.

1796, Nathaniel Maxey Pattison. .

1797, John Whitfield.

1798, Owen Lloyd.

1799, Samuel Williamson.

1800, James Twemlow.

1801, John Wilkinson.

1802, George Reade.

1803, Robert Hodgson.

1804, John Dean.

1805, John Johnson.

1806, Jonathan Broadhurst.

1807, John Wilkinson.

1809, Nathaniel Maxey Pattison.

1809, Holland Watson.

1810, James Twemlow.

1811, John Wilkinson.

1812, Samuel Williamson.

1813, Jonathan Broadhurst.

1814, Thomas Bowers.

1815, Jonathan Broadhurst.

1816, John Johnson

1817, John Skerratt.

1818, Thomas Bowers.

1819, Nath. Maxey Pattison.

List of the high stewards and their deputies, who have presided at the courts.

HIGH-STEWARDS

1624, Sir Thomas Savage, knight, and bart.

1627, Sir John Savage, bart.

1655, President Bradshaw,

1657, Thomas earl Rivers.

1714, James earl Barrymore.

1747, Thomas Furnivall, gent.

1749, John Crewe, jun'r, esq.

1752, Richard Wilbraham, esq.

1796, Rev. Richard Lowndes Salmon,

1798, Randle Wilbraham, esq.

DEPUTY-STEWARDS.

1575, Sir William Brereton.

1689, William Llandin, gent.

1595, Edward Savage, gent,

1596, Robert Colleigne, gent.

1689, Edward Thornicroft, gent.

1727, Thomas Bowyer, esq.

1749, Thomas Furnivall, gent.

1795, William Smith, gent. Edward E. Deacon, gent.

1814, John Lockett, gent.

THE GUILD-HALL.

This edifice is a handsome modern structure of brick, adorned with a colonnade in front, composed of four columns of stone, which support a piazza. The corporation in 1804, employed James Brown of Congleton, to pull down the old town-hall, which was a very ancient and inconvenient building, and rebuild it on a larger scale, according to an approved plan. He was to receive £630, and the old materials. The rooms connected with it were purchased for £ 70; thus the whole expenditure for the new edifice amounted to £700. It was finished in 1805. It contains a large room appropriated to the public business of the corporation; a jury-room; a room for the confinement of debtors; and dungeons for the temporary imprisonment of criminals, till they are either committed to the county jail at Chester, or the house of correction at Middlewich.

THE WORKHOUSE.

This edifice, erected through the exertions and in the mayoralty of Holland Watson, esq. in the year 1810, at an expense of about £3000, though not in the town, may properly be considered one of its public buildings. It is a commodious structure of brick; is situated on Congleton Moss, about half a mile from the town; is thirty-six yards long, ten yards broad, and eight yards high; and contains nineteen rooms. Two visitors are appointed monthly by the overseers, who visit the workhouse weekly, to examine the state of the inhabitants, and make whatever regulations they think requisite for their comfort and accommodation.

Though Congleton is in the parish of Astbury, it provides for its own poor; which, considering the size of the town, are always very numerous; but by virtue of an act of Parliament, passed in 1795, for the purpose of enclosing the commons or waste lands, within the borough and township; a portion of those lands were allotted for the use of the poor, as appears, from the following extract:—" That the money to arise from time to time by leasing or letting the said remainder of the said commons or waste grounds shall be applied and disposed of by the trustees, or any five or more of them, in the relief and maintenance of the poor of the said borough and township of Congleton, and in aid or ease, and in discharge (so far as the same will extend) of the poor rates within the same, in such manner as the said rates are directed to be disposed of and applied, and in case of any over- plus, the same shall from time to time be either kept as stock in hand, and be added to the next year's income, or shall be disposed of by the trustees, or any five or more of them, in aid of the highways, or other public expenses within the said borough and township of Congleton." These allotments of land, therefore, in their present cultivated state, are of considerable importance to the town, by reason of their making the poor's rates less burthensome than they otherwise would be. There are 49A. 2R. 22P. on Mossley Moss; 24A. OR. 3P. on Lower-Heath; and 105A. 1R. 39P. on West Heath— total, 179A. OR. 24P. The yearly rental is £649. The rates are collected in the township, about every three months, and have generally amounted, on a moderate rental, to four shillings in the pound.

The poor's rates of the township have been advanced more than tenfold since the year 1750, in that year they amounted to £300; in 1758, they were about £600. This great increase in eight years was occasioned by the influx of a multitude of indigent persons, who did not find sufficient support by the wages paid to them in the silk mills. In the year 1760, the poor's rates amounted to £600; in 1766, to about £680; in 1788, £1000; in 1800, £1300; in 1807, £2000; in 1809, nearly £2,400; and in 1814, they amounted to the enormous sum of £3000. By a late assessment, the poor's rates, including the rents of the common lands, are about £2339; one ley throughout the town amounts to £105, and there are about sixteen leys collected yearly. In 1765, there was a general survey made throughout the town, for the purpose of levying the poor rates in proportion to the property of individuals; and another general survey in 1819, when all the houses and land, in the township, were valued. From this calculation, a scale has been made by which the poor rates are collected.

The highway ley is sixpence in the pound, on the rent of houses and lands, and amounts to about £190.

REFERENCES

1. A statute so called, made 13 Edw. I. ann. 1285, ordaining the statute merchany; it was so termed from a place named Acton Burnel, where it was made; being a castle sometime belonging to the family of Burnel, and afterwards of Lovel, in Shropshire. Cowel.

2. The court of piepowder, or pie-poudre, is the lowest, but most expeditious court known to the law of England. Lord Coke attributes this name to the quality of justice being there administered as speedily as dust can fall from the foot. — According to Barrington, it is derived from pied puldreaux, (a pedlar in old French,) and therefore, signifying the court of such petty chapmen as resort to fairs and markets. It is court of record, incident to every fair or market; of which the steward of him, who owns or has the tolls of the market, is the judge; and its jurisdiction extends to administer justice for all commercial injuries done in that very fair or market, and not in any preceding one. So that the injury must be done, complained of, heard and determined, within the compass of one and the same day, unless the fair continue longer,". See Blackstone's Corn, 111. 83.

Detail - Church window

Congleton Church

CHAPTER IV
ECCLESIASTICAL AFFAIRS.

The Church, – Right of Nominating the Clegymen,
Monumental Inscriptions,
Extracts from the Parish Registers,
Unitarian Chapel, – Methodist Chapel, – Calvanist Chapel.

When Smith wrote his "Vale Royal," in the sixteenth century, there were two chapels in Congleton; one in the town, and the other near the bridge. They were distinguished by the names of the higher and the lower chapel, and were chapels of ease under the church of Astbury. Among the corporation papers are several bequests of rent or parts of the rent of small tenements and parcels of lands, towards the repair of the lower chapel. One of these bequests is dated 7. Edward IV. 1465, and is a grant from Roger Moreton, mayor of Congleton, of one half of a burgage, which produced the yearly rent of three shillings and four pence, "for the reparation and sustaining of the lower chapel and bridge in the said borough. Another grant from Ralph Pedley of eight pence, annually, being the rent of a parcel of land, for the above mentioned purpose. Under the article, expenditure, there is an entry of "sack and claret for Lord Brereton, when Brereton bells were cast in the old chapel in 1633." In illustration of this extract, however, it is asserted that the old chapel on the bridge, was converted into a bellfoundry[1], and afterwards into a workhouse. It is also to be observed that no memorandum remains of the name of any priest or minister who officiated in this chapel. The probability is, that 'it was a structure erected by some devotee, for the purpose of private devotion.

Of the existence of the higher chapel[2], or church of Congleton as a place of public worship for many ages there can be no doubt; but of its original foundation we have no record. That it was erected by the corporation seems clear, from the circumstance of its having always been supported out of its funds, and termed in the records, "our chapel of Congleton;" and that the power of nominating the minister was also vested in the corporation, as it still continues to be, notwithstanding some ineffectual attempts made from time to time by the rectors of Astbury to deprive them of this privilege.

In the year 1740, the higher chapel, or church, which was too small, and in rather a ruinous state, was pulled down; and in the course of the following year, a new church on a large scale, substantially built of brick, at the expense of about £2000, which was raised by voluntary subscription. The church consists of a nave and chancel, side aisles and galleries. There are two rows of six windows in each side; the lower ones small, and the upper large. The chancel is lighted by a large Venetian window. The tower contains six good bells[3], and a clock. The interior of the church is very neat and conveni ent, and kept exceedingly clean; the pews are of oak; the chancel is adorned with paintings of St. Paul and St. Peter, and other appropriate emblematic devises.

The corporation have always been tenacious of their privileges, and resisted every attempt, from whatever quarter, to infringe upon them. As they had for ages paid the salary of the minister they claimed the privilege of nominating to the curacy. This claim was by the advice and concurrence of the chancellors of London, York and Chester, adjudged by the bishop of the diocese, to be vested in the corporation, in the year 1698. Mr. Malbon afterwards elected by the corporation, was nominated by Mr. Hutchinson, rector of Astbury; and in 1722, upon the demise of Mr. Malbon, the dispute revived between the rector and the corporation, but the bishop nominated by lapse."

The appointment of Mr. Watwood by the bishop, did not, however, harmonize with the feelings of the corporation; and this gentleman, also seemed to consider himself as totally independent of them. This led to frequent contention, especially during the rebuilding the church; from that period, he would only preach once a day on Sunday. On the death of this clergyman in 1768, the corporation chose the reverend Richard Sandbach; but this gentleman also in the course of a few years became even more refractory than his predecessor. This conduct was deemed very ungrateful on the part of Mr. Sandbach, who had been chosen by the corporation, in opposition to the desire of Mr. Crewe, rector of Astbury, who claimed the right to nominate the minister of this chapel. This claim was resisted with great spirit; the cause was tried at the assizes at Chester, and the rector non-suited. It had been customary to invite the rector to preach an annual sermon in Congleton church on Care Sunday, after which he was entertained at the expense of the mayor; but after this lawsuit the invitation was discontinued.

Of the unaccommodating disposition of Mr. Sandbach, there is a memorable record in the corporation books, dated May 2nd, 1772, which states that, "Whereas Richard Sandbach, curate, claims the freehold of our chapel of Congleton, and insists upon it, that no person hath any right to bury their dead in our said chapel, or to erect any monument in said chapel or chapel-yard: and hath taken of the representatives of the late Richard Webster, alderman, the sum of ten shillings and sixpence, for his consent to bury the corpse of the said Richard Webster, in the said chapel:—Ordered, that no person shall bury their dead in our said chapel, or chapel yard, without our license and consent: and that the said Richard Sandbach shall have notice of the said order, and that a councellor's opinion shall be had thereon."

Occasional contentions appear to have existed between the corporation and their minister for several years, and from the following record Mr. Sandbach appears to have been a very negligent, if not a contumacious clergyman:—April 12th, 1776, Thomas Yearsley, mayor, "R. Sandbach having refused to visit sick people, and privately to baptize weak sickly infants, the mayor and justices for the time being, are appointed a committee to manage, prosecute, and carry on a presentment against him in the ecclesiastical court." This disputation terminated in the removal of Mr. Sandbach in the year 1785, when the corporation appointed the reverend Samuel Williamson, the present minister, as his successor.

The minister's income from this church, including his stipend, official house, and surplice fees, was returned by the bishop of this diocese, February 13th, 1809, to be £126 6s. 10d.

The sunday-school belonging to the established church, is situated on Cowhill-bank; it is a plain building of brick, erected in the year 1809, at the expense of the corporation; and upwards of three hundred children receive instruction in this school, according to the approved system of education invented by Dr. Bell.

In the year 1726, the sum of one hundred pounds was voted by the corporation, for the purpose of erecting a new parsonage house.

Before the year 1686, the inhabitants buried their dead at Astbury. The following are the most remarkable monumental inscriptions in this church.

A marble mural monument in the nave, inscribed:

SACRED
To the Memory of ELIZABETH widow of
JOHN ALSAGER of ALSAGER; Gentleman,
who died March the 18th, 1750, in the 72d. year of her age :

Also of ANN their Daughter, who died Jan. the 19th.
1743, in the 40th year of her Age;

also of JOHN ALSAGER, esq. their Son,
who died Jan. 22. 1768, in the 54th year of his Age;

Also of JOHN & RALPH their Sons,
who died in their Infancy;

Also of their Daughters,
SARAH, who died July 11. 1769,
aged 61;
ELIZABETH, April 4 1783, 77
MARGARET, May 13. 1789, 72;
JUDITH, Feb. 21, 1795, 75;
MARY, Mar. 23, 1795, 82.
Arms. Ermine, on a chief three lions rampant.

A tablet, annexed to a pillar on the opposite side of the nave, bears the following inscription :

Over
against this pillar in the middle
Isle lyeth interred the body
of John Smith, Late Alderman,
and twice Mayor of the
town, he gave the Chandelier
and was other Ways a
benefactor to the Church.
he died on the 30 January, 1749
Aged 59.

On a marble tablet in the south aisle :

Here lyeth. Interr'd
the Body of SAMUEL PATTISON, late of London, Merchant:
a Person of Unspotted Integrity, of Exemplary Virtue, and
Endow'd with every Amiable Quality that can Adorn
Human Nature,
Therefore Universally Regretted by his Family and Friends!
He resided during a Year before his Death, in this Town
As DIRECTOR of the SILK MILLS,
where by his great Abilitys, and Unwearied Application,
he render'd the most important Services :
and Enjoy'd the Satisfaction of Living to See all the Works Compleated,
and the Manufacture brought to perfection.
Obit. 27 May, 1756, Æt. 30.

The following is on a very neat marble tablet adjoining :

Sacred to the Memory of HELEN
wife of NATHANIEL MAXEY PATTISON, of this borough, Esq.
who died the 6, day of November 1818, in the 55th year of her age.
Of thee blest Saint bereft We Mourn to whom impoverished Life is left,
Mourn for ourselves! Secure thy lot must be,
With those who pure in Heart their GOD shall see.

On a brass plate in the same aisle :

In Memory
of James Starkey,
of Darley, esq. who
Departed this life the
ninth day of December, in
the seventy ninth year of his age,
anno Domini 1728.
In well grounded hopes of a blessed resurrection to life eternal
the mortal remains of Katherine,
wife of James Starkey, esq.
were underneath deposited Jany. 23, 1718.

On a brass tablet in the north aisle :

Near to this place are Interred the Bodies of four Children
of John and Susanna Sydebotham of this Town, viz :
Susanna who dyed August the 31st, 1727
Ann who dyed January the 16th, 1727
Peter who dyed January the 25th 1734

Jane who dyed October the 9th, 1755.
And also John Kirkby, Druggist their Son- in-law
who dyed October the 6th, 1759
Mary Bagnall, their Grand Daughter December 14, 1769
The aforesaid John Sydebotham, March 25 Aged 78.
Susanna, his Wife, March 10, 1774 Aged 77.
Susanna Kirkby, Widow, died Oct. 17, 1812 Aged 81.

On a monument in the same aisle is the following inscription:

In a vault near this place
are interred the remains of HARRIOTT, wife of HOLLAND WATSON,
ESQUIRE,
who died on the 16th of March, 1819, aged 50 years.

This Monument is erected by her greatly afflicted Husband to perpetuate
the memory of one of the best of wives.

The following inscriptions are on tombs in the burial ground; the
first of which is the oldest tomb in this ground.

Dum amici
Johannis Brooke
de Condate Coriarij nono
die Septembris morientis,
Anno 1688 Lachrymis
Sepulchrum inspiciunt,
Spe lætantur.

Mors piis œrumnarum requies.

Thomas
Thomæ Malbon,
Condatensis filius
natu maximus 33 An-.
nos cum natus esset 4to.
et 20 mo Aprilis die 1689
mortalitatem deposiut.
In Memory of the
Rev. J. Wilson, Vicar of Biddulph, and
33 years Master of the Grammar School in Congleton,
the duties of which situation he discharged
with Great ability, diligence and
usefulness. He died Jan. 17th 1810.
Aged 61 years.

Baptisms and burials.

	Baptisms,	Burials.
1812 —	133 —	58
1813 —	112 —	74
1814 —	145 —	103
1815 —	138 —	71
1816 —	133 —	108
1817 —	125 —	77
1818 —	160 —	76

Presbeterian or Unitarian Chapel (mill street)

PRESBYTERIAN CHAPEL.

The meeting house of the Presbyterians, was founded in the year 1687, at that memorable period of our history, when the priest-ridden bigot James, employed every machination that cunning could devise, to subvert the Protestant religion in England. It was opened with a funeral sermon, on the death of the reverend George Moxon, formerly curate of Astbury, but ejected by the statute against non-conformity, enacted on the accession of Charles the second, in 1660.

Mr. Moxon then came to reside in Congleton, and took out a license to preach in the house which he rented near Dane bridge, at the end of mill-street. Here he preached occasionally to a small congregation till the year 1687, when he died of the palsy, at the age of 85 years. The Presbyterians continued to meet in this house till the death of Queen Anne, in 1714, when it was demolished, and the pulpit and seats destroyed by a mob of tories, as we have already mentioned.

The present small but neat edifice was erected on the west side of mill-street, by contributions collected by some opulent dissenters in Congleton and Buglawton; but the congregation continued small, and the income was insufficient for the maintenance of a minister. In 1802, the reverend Thomas Jones of Middlewich, preached here once every month, but he soon afterwards discontinued his monthly visit, and the chapel was closed for some years.

The Unitarians took possession of this chapel in the year 1812, and since that time divine service has been regularly solemnized there. There is a small sunday-school belonging to this class sectarians, in which about one hundred and fifty boys and girls, receive gratuitous instruction.

METHODIST CHAPEL

This large and handsome modern edifice is built of brick, with an adjoining house for the accommodation of the preacher. It is situated in wagg-street; and the sunday-school, belonging to the society, which joins the chapel, was built in the year 1818, by public subscription. The school-rooms are sufficiently spacious to contain one thousand scholars, and there are now upwards of seven hundred children instructed in this institution.

Methodism was first promulgated in Congleton by the venerable founder, John Wesley, accompanied by his brother Charles; the former preached at Congleton-cross, in the year 1746. Its progress in this town and neighbourhood has been steady and successful.

Galvanist Chapel Mill street

CALVINIST CHAPEL.

This edifice is situated in mill-street. It was built at the sole expense of the late reverend John Scott; was finished and opened in December, 1790; and left by the founder, in trust, for the use of the Calvinists. Adjoining to the chapel, a sunday-school was built by subscription in the year 1810, in which nearly two hundred children receive instruction.

THE GRAMMAR SCHOOL.

This institution though last described here, is the first on record in the corporation books. It was founded and endowed by the corporation in the sixteenth century, and remains an honourable monument of the liberality and public spirit of our ancestors, in that truly memorable and glorious æra when the illustrious Elizabeth held the sceptre of England.

The schoolhouse is situated to the south of the church, on the highest ground in the church- yard, and near the south-east angle of that enclosure. The first record of its existence is dated 1590, in the mayoralty of Matthew Moreton, when different sums were paid for the furniture of the schoolroom, and the schoolmaster's wages, amounting to £14. 7s. The master's salary at that time was £13. 6s. 8d. it has since been increased to £16, with a house, garden, and close of land containing one acre, rent free. The schoolmaster is also paid the interest of £20 per annum, given to the institution by Mr Hulme in 1736. A new and commodious schoolroom was erected near the scite of the former, in 1814, at the expense of the corporation, with the following inscription over the entrance:

CONDITA,

J. BROADHURST. ARMIG:

PRÆT: MUNICIP:

A.D.MDCCCXIV.

Of the abilities and attention of the several masters appointed to this school, we have frequent mention in the corporation books. The late reverend Jonathan Wilson is particularly noticed for the many essential services which he from time to time rendered his townsmen. He translated the charters of the borough into English; arranged the records in chronological order; and his pen and advice were ever ready to contribute to the welfare of the inhabitants. For these public services he was remunerated by the corporation with ten guineas, and had the freedom of the borough conferred upon him as a mark of the esteem of his brother-burgesses. Mr. Wilson was a man of considerable literary attainment; he published an improved grammar of the English language, and produced several other useful school books.

On his demise in 1810, his kinsman, the reverend Edward Wilson was appointed to succeed him. The grammar school is free only to the sons of burgesses, but Mr. Wilson also receives into his house a limited number of pupils.

REFERENCES

1. It is mentioned by Bishop Gastrell in 1724, as having been then lately repaired. Notitia Cestriensis.

2. The following bequest is the earliest document, in which mention is made of the church or higher chapel, we have been able to discover among the corporation records. "Grant from Philip Green of Congleton, and John Yates, executors of the will of Robert Biddulph, clerk, unto Mason, his heirs and assigns, of one burgage, with its appurtenances, lying within the borough of Congleton, near Parklane, and one parcel with the buildings and appurtenances to the same belonging, subject to the payment of the yearly rent of three shillings, by equal portions on the Feast of St. Martin, and the Nativity of St. John the Baptist, unto Philip Greene, mayor, of the borough of Congleton, and his successors, towards the building, repairing, and amending of the higher chapel of Congleton, with power of distress and re-entry in case of default in payment thereof. Dated the 1st Monday of the Feast of St. Gregory. 14, Henry IV." A D. 1413.

3. The words Nolæ and Campaneæ, given to bells used in churches, are said to have originated in the circumstance of church-bells being first invented by Paulinus, Bishop of Nola in Campania, about the year 400. Hist. of Uxbridge. The people were first called together to prayers, at stated hours in the day, by the sound of a bell, by a decree of Pope Sabinian, the successor of St. Gregory. Faulkner's Fulham

Bells in the time of popery, were baptized, anointed 'Oleo Chrismatis,' exorcised and blessed by the Bishop; these and other ceremonies ended, it was believed that they had the power to drive the devil out of the air, calm storms and tempests, make fair weather, extinguish sudden fires, and raise the dead. Weever's Fun. Mon. p. 118.

The dislike of spirits to bells is thus mentioned in the Golden Legend of Wynken de Worde: "It is said the evil spirytes, that ben in the regon of thayre, doubte moche when they here the belles rongen; and this is the cause why the bells ben rongen whan it thondreth, and whan grete tempests and outrages of whether happen; to the ende that the fiends and wyched spirytes shold be abashed and flee, and cease of the movynge of tempeste."

Old Dane Bridge Bridge and Man Length 140 foot width 6 foot aD 1750

Old Dane Bridge

CHAPTER V.
MANUFACTURES.

Linen and Woollen Weavers, – Glovers, – Congleton Points,
Silk Throwing First Introduced,
List of Silk Throwsters In and Near Congleton,
Cotton Manufactures, – Ribbon Weavers.

The first manufactures of Congleton, like all other communities were those arising from necessity, or the common handicraft arts. Linen and woollen weavers, skinners, and glovers, were among the first handicraftsmen who settled here, and supplied the town and neighbourhood with the productions of their skill and ingenuity. Afterwards a new branch of manufacture constituted the staple commodity of the borough. This was the celebrated "Congleton points." They were made of tough white leather, cut into small thongs, and pointed at the ends with tags made of tin or silver, similar to those now used for womens' laces. Congleton points were generally worn for ages, by men and women. All the men's garments were tied with them, and they were also used by the women instead of the bodkins and skewers formerly worn. The points continued fashionable and in great demand till the invention of buckles and buttons, the latter of which, particularly those manufactured with so much beauty at Birmingham, completely superseded them.

Of the modern manufactures by which Congleton has risen to so high a degree of opulence, elegance, and refinement, that of silk is the principal. The idea of establishing the silk throwing business in this town was first suggested by — Pattison, esq., an opulent silk merchant of London, who, being desirous to have an establishment of this kind connected with his other commercial concerns, placed his son Mr. Nathaniel Pattison, under the tuition of Richard Wilson, esq., the then proprietor of the celebrated mill at Derby[1], and agreed with Mr. John Clayton, silk throwster of Stockport, to contract for a suitable piece of ground on the river Dane, for the purpose of erecting a silk-mill. Accordingly the workhouse garden, situated on the northern bank of the Dane, was leased from the corporation for a term of years. When Mr. Pattison had gained a knowledge of the machinery, and perfected himself in the art of throwing silk, he occasionally resided in Congleton to superintend the works till 1754; when his brother Samuel Pattison, esq. came to conduct the affairs of the mill, which he brought to perfection in 1755. But he was soon removed from the scene of usefulness which he had established, for he died of a fever in this town in 1756, in the 30th year of his age, and was interred in the church, where there is a monument with an appropriate inscription erected to his memory.

The first silk-mill, which is yet the largest and most conspicuous structure in Congleton, is built of brick, with a pediment, containing the dial plate of the clock in the centre. It is 240 feet long, twenty-four feet wide, and forty-eight feet high, consisting of five stories; and is lighted by 390 windows. Three of the rooms contain seventy-five winding engines, which perform 32,850 movements. Their office is to draw off or wind upon a small cylindrical block of wood, or bobbin, the raw silk, which is placed on an hexagonal wheel called the swift. The other two rooms contain the cleaning engines, and the spinning, doubling, and throwing mills. The cleaning engines wind the silk from the first set of bobbins on to another; in this part of the process many children are employed, whose nimble fingers are kept in continual exercise by tying the threads that break. The cleaning engines are twenty-one in number, and perform 3,150 movements. The spinning and throwing mills were originally of a circular form, and were turned by upright shafts, passing through their centres, and communicating with shafts from the water-wheel; their diameter was between twelve and fourteen feet; and their height about nineteen feet. These were, a few years ago, taken down, and replaced by machinery of a more modern construction, by means of which nearly double the quantity of silk can be spun in the same space. There are thirty-eight spinning mills, which perform 39,520 movements. The spindles run in steps of glass, and the threads are conducted over glass rods from one bobbin to another. There are twenty-two doubling engines, which have 6,820 movements. There are likewise upwards of sixty women employed in doubling silk on single wheels. The throwing mills, which wind the silk from the bobbins upon reels, and form it again into skeins ready for the dyers, perform 11,076 movements. The total number of movements is 115,600, and the number of wheels is 21,116.

The whole of this elaborate machine, for one only it is, although distributed through five large rooms, is put in motion by a single water wheel nineteen feet, six inches, in diameter, and five feet, six inches broad, situated in the centre of the building. The wheel is regulated to go and keep time with a clock, by a contrivance that admits more or less water upon the wheel, so as always to make the motion uniform. The timepiece, worked by means of the wheel, does not vary a minute, in the course of the day, from the common clock.

"An adequate idea of this complicated assemblage of wheels cannot be conveyed by words; to be distinctly conceived, it must be seen; and even then considerably more time is requisite to obtain a knowledge of its parts, and of their dependence on each other, than is generally allotted by a casual visitant. All is whirling and in motion, and appears as if directed and animated by some invisible power; yet mutually dependent as every part is, any one of them may be stopped and separated at pleasure. This arises from every movement being performed by two wheels, one of which is turned by the other; but when separated, the latter preserves its rotatory motion, while the other stops as the impelling power no longer operates[2].

The present proprietors are Nathaniel Maxey Pattison esq. of Congleton; James Pattison, esq. of London, and Mr. James Pattison, son of the former gentleman; who constantly employ, in this extensive establishment, upwards of four hundred persons, including men, women, and children .

The success of the projectors of this silk-mill, induced others to engage in the same business; and in a few years several silk throwsters erected silk-mills on a smaller scale; some of which on the banks of the Dane, and the brook Howty, are worked by water; and others, in the town, and neighbourhood, are worked by steam.

There are several other silk-mills on the river Dane, which are of considerable magnitude, particularly the one belonging to Messrs Hall and Johnson, at Daneinshaw, in which upwards of 200 persons are employed; in the vicinity of this silk-mill a number of cottages have been recently erected by the proprietors, for the accommodation of the people employed in the mill.

The silk-mills of Messrs William and Thomas Johnson, of Throstles-nest, and Mr. Henry Hogg, of Near Daneinshaw, are very extensive.

The following is an accurate list of all the silk throwsters in and near the town.
Barlow Charles Daneinshaw,
Barlow Elizabeth, bridge-street
Barlow George, west-street,
Barlow Paul, west-street,
Boyse Samuel, lawton-street,
Booth Allen, bridge-street,
Broadhurst James, Daneinshaw,
Broadhurst John, Dane mill,
Cotton John, lawton-street,
Daniel John, Cowhill-bank,
Duncalf John, mill-street,
Edwards Richard, booth-street,
Foden James, west-street,
Forster, William and son, wagg-street,
Gent and Norbury, moody-street,
Gent Peter, chapel-street,
Hackney Charles, lawton-street,
Hall and Johnson, Daneinshaw,
Hall John, dane-street,

Hall Richard, mill-street

Harthern Thomas, bridge-street,

Hogg Henry, Daneinshaw,

Hulme James, booth-street,

Jackson John, moody-street,

Jefferis and Cockson, Havannah mills,

Johnson John, Daneinshaw,

Johnson William and Thomas, Throstles-nest,

Johnson James, bridge-street,

Lockett Charles, mill-street,

Pattison, N. M., J. and J. Congleton silk-mills.

Pedley and Thornicroft, mill-street,

Roe Charles and Co. Dane mill,

Roe George, bridge-street,

When the cotton manufacture in all its branches was established in Lancashire, to the great emolument of the manufacturers, and the advancement of national commerce, the business was gradually introduced by enterprizing men into Cheshire, and other counties.

In the year 1784, Mr. Richard Martin established the spinning of cotton in this town; and soon afterwards Messrs George and William Reade, Mr. Jesse Drakeford, and Mr. John Vaudrey, began the same business here. The machinery for spinning cotton at first consisted of the simple instrument called a jenny, but in 1790, when Sir Richard Arkwright's improvements in machinery were universally adopted by cotton spinners, the mule superceded the jenny. At present there are three large establishments of this kind in Congleton and its neighbourhood, namely, that of Mr. Reade; Mr. Vaudrey, of Buglawton; and Mr. Jesse Drakeford.

The manufacture of ribbons for the Coventry merchants was established in the year 1755. It was carried on to a considerable extent for about forty years, and afforded employment to many industrious ribbon-weavers; but since 1790, it has gradually declined. Messrs Gent, and Norbury, Mr. James Foden, and Mr. Richard Edwards, are the only ribbon manufacturers in this town, who carry on that business to any extent.

REFERENCES

1. As the following account of the introduction of the silk-mill into England essentially varies from almost every other that has been published on the subject, it becomes expedient to mention, that the chief authority on which it is related, is the 'History of Derby,' by Mr. Hutton. This gentleman was personally known to GARTREVALLI; and in his infancy was well acquainted with the names both of the other Italian, and of the female to whose arts John Lombe fell a victim; but the lapse of threescore years, as he observes, in a letter with which he has favored us, 'has driven them out of his mind.' Various particulars of his statement we have substantiated by local inquiries, and by referring to original documents; from which some particulars are inserted in the text, that Mr. Hutton was probably unacquainted with. Beauties of England, vol. Ill. p. 368.

"The original mill, called the Silk-mill to denote its pre-eminence, being the first and largest of its kind ever erected in England, stands upon an island in the river Derwent. Its history is remarkable, as it denotes the power of genius, and the vast influence which even the enterprizes of an individual has on the commerce of a country.

"The Italians were long in the exclusive possession of the art of silk throwing, and the merchants of other nations were consequently dependent on that people for their participation in a very lucrative article of trade, and were frequently deprived of their fair profits by exorbitant prices charged for the original material. This state of things continued till the commencement of the last century, when a person named Crotchet erected a small mill near the present works, with an intention of introducing the silk manufacture into England; but his machinery being inadequate to the purpose, he quickly became insolvent, and the design was for some time abandoned. At length, about the year 1715, a similar idea began to expand in the mind of an excellent mechanic and draughtsman, named John Lombe, who, though young, resolved on the perilous task of travelling into Italy, to procure drawings, or models of the machines necessary for the undertaking.

"In Italy he remained some time; but, as admission to the silk works was prohibited, he could only obtain access by corrupting two of the workmen, through whose assistance he inspected the machinery in private, and whatever parts he obtained a knowledge of, during these visits, he recorded on paper before he slept. By perseverance in this mode of conduct, he made himself acquainted with the whole; and had just completed his plan, when his intention was discovered, and his life being in extreme hazard, he flew with precipitation, and took refuge on ship-board. The two Italians who had favored his scheme, and whose lives were in equal danger with his own, accompanied him, and they all soon landed in safety in England: this happened about the year 1717.

"Fixing on Derby as a proper place for his purpose, he agreed with the corporation for an island, or swamp, in the river, 500 feet long, and 52 wide, at a rent somewhat below eight pounds yearly. Here he established his silk-mill; but during the time employed in its construction, he erected temporary machines in the Town-Hall, and various other places; by which means he not only reduced the prices of silk far below the Italians, but was likewise enabled to proceed with his greater undertaking, though the charges amounted to nearly £30,000.

"In the year 1718, he procured a patent to enable him to secure the profits, thus arising from his address and ingenuity, for the term of fourteen years; but his days verged to a close, and before half this period had elapsed, treachery and poison had brought him to the grave. The Italians, whose trade rapidly decreased, from the success of the new establishment, were exasperated to vengence, and vowed the destruction of the man whose ingenuity had thus turned the current of their business into another channel. An artful woman was sent from Italy in the character of a friend; she associated with the parties, and was permitted to assist in the preparation of the silk. Her influence was privately exerted on the natives who had fled with Mr. Lombe from Italy, and succeeding with one, she prepared to execute the long meditated plan of death. The victim lingered in agony two or three years, when the springs of life being completely exhausted, he breathed his last. Slow poison is supposed to have been the means employed to deprive him of existance; and though suspicion was almost strengthened into certainty, by the circumstances that transpired on the examination of Madam, the evidence was not decisive, and she was discharged. Her associate had previously ran away to his own country. The other Italian, whose name was Gartrevalli, continued in Derby, and afterwards went to Stockport; but he died in poverty. The funeral of John Lombe was celebrated in a style of considerable magnificence."

2. Descrip. of silk-mill at Derby.

Little Moreton Hall

CHAPTER VI.
CHARITABLE INSTITUTIONS.

Benevolent Society, – Bible Society,
Sunday-Schools, – Sick Clubs, – Savings Bank,
Benefactions and Charities

Among the charitable institutions of Congleton, that denominated "The Benevolent institution for visiting and relieving poor sick persons and married lying-in-women at their own habitations," is particularly worthy of approbation. The following extract from the secretary's last report, will sufficiently shew to what extent this institution has proved beneficial in meliorating the condition of the poor: "From the beginning of September, 1818, to the end of August, 1819, it appears from the books, that three hundred and forty-seven individuals have been visited and relieved;—the total number of visits to the abodes of sickness and poverty being upwards of fifteen hundred; and the money thus distributed amounting to £86, 7s. 6d."

A Bible society, constituting a branch of the Chester Society, was established here in November, 1812. As the annual reports of the committee have been printed and circulated among the subscribers, it will be unnecessary to give an extended account of the proceedings of the society. The committee in their first report observe, "That within so small a compass as the sphere of the Congleton branch Bible Society, there were 790 families without a Bible; and 393 families (consisting of 1845 individuals) who did not possess even a single leaf of the word of God."—The total number of books distributed by the society, appears from the sixth report to be 1400 Bibles, and 362 Testaments.

There are four sunday-schools in this town; and though each is under the immediate patronage and management of a particular sect of christians, let it be recorded to the honor of the philanthropy of the inhabitants, that in the truly benevolent spirit of evangelical christianity, they liberally contribute to the support of all. The number of children instructed in the four sunday-schools, amounts to one thousand three hundred. The following paragraph, extracted from the first report of the Bible society, is explanatory of the utility of these institutions, and will testify, upon the best authority, the excellence of sunday-schools. "Since the general institution of sunday-schools, the number of poor families who have no individual among them that can read is comparatively small. In proof of which, your committee beg leave to state, that out of 519 poor families visited in the town of Congleton, there are only twenty-one without some person who can read the Bible."

There are seven sick clubs, or friendly societies in this town; a savings bank has been recently opened for the security of the property acquired by the industrious and frugal; and on a general view of society, perhaps no town in the united kingdom possesses more local and other advantages, or is more exempt from grievances than that of Congleton.

The following charitable donations appear by a table in the town-hall, to be vested in the corporation, the yearly interest of which is given in money to poor housekeepers, on St. Thomas' day, along with Parnell's charity.

	Amount.			Annual produce.		
Samuel Malbon	50	0	0	2	10	0
Jane Davies	50	0	0	2	10	0
Mr. Jolley	16	0	0	0	16	0
Mr. Wilkinson	5	0	0	0	5	0
Dr.Dean	5	0	0	0	5	0
Mrs. Buckley	2	0	0	0	2	0
Mr. Hancock	1	10	0	0	1	6
Mr.Jackson	1	0	0	0	1	0
Mr.Smith	5	0	0	2	5	3
Mr.Bellot	5	0	0	2	5	3

Robert Hodgson, by deed, dated July 31, 1790.

To be given to six poor house-keepers not paupers. 3   0   0

Robert Hulme, by will, dated Aug. 5, 1708.

To the master of the grammar school   20   0   0

                                 1   0   0

BENEFACTIONS AND CHARITIES,

Relating to the corporation, minister, schoolmaster, and overseers of Congleton.

By whom given.	When given, and whether by will or deed.	For what purpose given.	Whether in land or money, and in whom now invested.	Amount if in money.	Annual produce.
William Parnell	1622, 13, July. by will	Bread weekly&money on St. Thomas' day	A charge on lands in Bug-lawton; mayor & ald'r'n		5 6 0
Ralph Stubbs	1661, 4, Oct. by will	In bread weekly ..	A charge on a house in chapel-st; mayor & ald.		2 12 0
Dame eliz Booth	1622, 20, Dec. by deed	In bread, weekly**	In money; mayor, Aldn, and cap. burg. given by the overseers	100 0 0	5 0 0
Dr. Dean	.... by will	Pious uses.‡	May'r, jus. & sen. alder.		63 0 0
Samuel Moreton	1727, 28, Aug. by will	Bread on Whitsunday	In money ; overseers ..	20 0 0	1 0 0
Josiah Cragg..	1761, 6, June, by deed	In money..........	Houses in Congleton ; 4, 5, & 6, cap. burgesses		18 18 0
Joseph Staton	1773, 15, Mar. by will	Given in shoes, stock-ings, shirts & shifts§	In money ; the mayor, aldermen, & burgesses, with the overseers....	400 0 0	16 0 0
John Holford..	1712, 24, Feb. by deed	For the support of poor persons, or put-ting out apprentices not paupers.†	In lands in Astbury ; John Egerton, esq. ..		120 0 0

* Half of this is given at Astbury, and half at Congleton; the corporation add two shillings annually to the latter; and Astbury the same to the former. † One third part of this is distributed by the minister of Congleton alone, to such objects of charity as he and the rector of Astbury should think fit. ‡ Clothes for poor persons. § To poor boys and girls.

CHAPTER VII.
Charters, – Grants, &c.

The charters and records of the borough are all in a state of high preservation; the seals of the greater part of them being perfect.

A TRANSLATION OF HENRY LACY'S CHARTER.

Know all men present and to come, that we, Henry de Lascy[1], earl of Lincoln, and constable of Chester, have given, granted, and by this our present charter have confirmed, for us and our heirs, to our free burgesses of Congleton, that the said town may be a free borough, and that the burgesses of the same borough may have at their pleasure for ever, a guild merchant[2], with all liberties and free customs to such a guild appertaining. They also may have housebote and haybote and common of pasture for all their beasts and cattle, every where within our territory of Congleton, with unlimited fuel, without the deliverance of any one on our part when they shall need, as of turves and peats, to be digged, dried, and taken anywhere in the turbary of Congleton. And that they shall be quit of pannage, how many hogs soever they shall have within the bounds of Congleton. And that by virtue of a charter of grant and confirmation of the liberties of our boroughs, which we have from

133

our sovereign lord the king, they are acquitted for ever throughout all places in Cheshire as well by land as by water, under the defence and protection of us and our heirs, with all their merchandises from toll, stallage, passage, pavage[3], pontage[4], lastage[5], and murage[6], and from all other impeachments which touch merchandises, except reasonable amends, if they commit trespass. And that they may not be impleaded, nor adjudged, out of their own proper borough, of any plea concerning their lands and tenements, nor of any plea which sounds as a transgression committed within the limits of the said town. And if any one of them in our mercy, shall fall by default, it may not exceed twelvepence, and after judgement, a reasonable amerciament according to the quantity of the offence. And that they shall grind their grist at our mill of Congleton at the twentieth grain, while the mill shall be sufficient. And that our burgesses aforesaid may choose for themselves, by themselves, a mayor and catchpole, and ale-taster, and shall present them at the appearance of our great court there, upon Tuesday next after the Feast of St. Michael; and our bailiff shall take their oath, for their faithful service to the lord and commonality. Also, we grant for us, our heirs and assigns that the aforesaid burgesses, their heirs and assigns, may have their burgages, and lands pertaining to their burgages, and also the lands which within the aforesaid lordship may reasonably be approved or rented[7], by oath of the aforesaid burgesses, without hurt of their liberty or their common aforesaid and hold them peaceably and quietly for ever, to wit, every burgage for sixpence yearly, and every acre of land for twelvepence, at the accustomed rent days. And that they make to our court three appearances yearly, at days certain. Yet a writ of right[8] issuing in the said court, they shall do suit from fortnight to fortnight, for all other manner of services and demands. And that their burgages and lands aforesaid they may lawfully sell, give, mortgage, or alienate as they please, except to religious persons. And that if the bailiffs of the town shall take any felon, the felony being known, they may lawfully behead him, and the felony being unknown, they shall hold him (if they will) in the stocks for three days, and afterward shall send him to our castle of Halton with the chattels found with him, saving to them the pelf which belongs to the serjeants. And we, Henry and our heirs all the aforesaid liberties, burgages, lands, and tenements with all their appurtenances, and free usages of the said town to the aforesaid burgesses , their heirs, and assigns, against all people, will, warrant, acquit and for ever defend. In witness whereof to this present charter our seal we have put, these being witnesses, John Deyville, William le Vavasour, Robert of Stokeport, Geffery of Chedle, knights; Richard of Rode, Gralam of Tideby, Bertam of Saxeby, Vincent of Wombwelle, Gervase a clergyman, and, others." There is no date to this charter. Henry Lacy died in the year 1310.

Henry the eighth granted an exemplification of Henry Lacy's charter, and nearly in the same words, except that "housebote, haybote and unlimited fuel, and beheading a felon," were omitted. Dated July 15th, 1518.

Another exemplification of the same was granted May 4th, 1533. It does not appear for what purpose these two exemplifications, by inspeximus, were applied for or granted; they neither abolish the parts left out, nor confirm what is retained.

The same king grants an injunction or mandate, for exempting the inhabitants from appearing at other courts. Dated June 15th, 1524.

James the first granted an exemplification of the above injunction, October 31st, 1608. There is also a recitation of this and of another by Elizabeth in the 43d, year of her reign and a confirmation of them by James the first, dated June 15th, 1612.— Henry the eighth granted an injunction, in the same words, dated April 26th, 1532, which does not appear to have been enrolled.

Henry the sixth, by charter, bearing date June 29th, 1451, granted the corn mills to the mayor and commonality of Congleton; and also an injunction on the 16th of November in the same year, that no other mills should be erected in the lordship of Congleton.— This injunction is in English.

Philip and Mary granted a decree that only resident freemen

should have votes in choosing the mayor and other officers. May 20th, 1556.

Elizabeth confirmed and ratified sundry records and decrees, June 9th, 1578.

The same queen granted a charter to the burgesses, January 23d. 1583. This charter confirms and ratifies all the "privileges and hereditaments already granted and held by them"; and by it they are empowered to make bye-laws, and punish offenders by fine and imprisonment.

The same queen granted an exemplification of a decree respecting the town-wood and the corporation lands; and also about ulnage and the fishing of Dane. Dated February 16th, 1583.

The same queen granted a mandamus to the inhabitants, which exempts them from paying tolls in all markets, fairs, and places in England, under the penalty of £100, to be forfeited by the person, or persons who shall demand or take any thing for the same. Dated June 21st, 1585.

James the first granted a new charter to the borough. This charter is the one under which the corporation act, and for its length and importance may be termed their Magna Charta, of which the following is an accurate translation freed from technical redundancies.

"James, by the grace of God, king of England, France and

Ireland, &c.: To all to whom these presents shall come, greeting, Whereas our town of Congleton is a very ancient and populous town, and has had many franchises and privileges granted and confirmed by divers kings and queens of England, to its inhabitants and officers, under different names. And that it shall be from henceforth a free borough of itself, one one body corporate and politic by the name of "The mayor, aldermen, and burgesses of the borough of Congleton, in the county of Chester," and that by the same name they may have perpetual succession. And under that name may and shall be for ever persons fit and capable in law, to have and hold lands, tenements, liberties, and other hereditaments, in fee and perpetuity, and also to give, grant, demise, or let the same. And that by the same name they may plead and be impleaded, may defend and be defended, in any courts, pleadings, and places. And that they may have a common seal to serve for transacting any of their own or successors, causes or affairs to be broken or changed at pleasure. And that there may and shall be one of the burgesses of the said borough, dwelling and residing within the said borough, chosen mayor, and that eight of the burgesses shall be chosen aldermen, and sixteen of the burgesses be chosen capital burgesses, which aldermen and capital burgesses shall be of the common council, and shall from time to time be aiding and assisting the mayor in all affairs concerning the said borough. And the mayor, aldermen, and capital-burgesses, or the greater part of them, (the mayor and two justices be three) collected by public summons, shall have power to make laws, statutes, and orders in writing, for the good rule and government of the said borough and all its inhabitants, and for victualling the same. And shall appoint fines and punishments to enforce the observation of them, and may levy and have the said fines to the use of the said mayor, aldermen, and capital burgesses, All of which laws and ordinances, shall be observed under the penalties contained in the same; yet, so that such laws and ordinances be reasonable, and not repugnant nor contrary to the laws and statutes of the realm. And for the better execution of our will, we name and make our beloved Philip Oldfield, esq. to be the first and modern mayor of the said borough, and to continue in office till the Monday next before St. Michael, and till another be sworn. We, also, nominate and make our beloved John Hobson, Edward Drakeford, Randle Rode, John Latham the elder, Matthew Holiday, Thomas Parnel, Roger Poynton, and William Newton, to be the first and modern aldermen, who shall continue in office during life, unless displaced by the mayor, aldermen, and capital burgesses, for some default. We will also, that the said mayor and aldermen, shall choose so many of the more reputable and discreet freemen, inhabiting and residing within the said borough, not exceeding the number of sixteen, as shall seem most expedient, to be the first and modern capital burgesses, who shall continue in office during life, unless displaced by the mayor and common council. And further our will is, that the mayor aldermen, capital-burgesses, and freemen, shall choose every year, for ever, on Monday next before the Feast of St. Michael, the archangel, one of the aldermen to be mayor of the said borough, for one whole year, and before he is admitted to execute his office, he shall take the oath before the last preceding mayor, or his deputy, or two or more aldermen; and that after such his oath so taken, he may have power to execute the said office, and to continue in the same one year, unless he die or be displaced by the common-council. And that if the mayor shall die or be displaced, (for it is our will that the mayor be removeable for a reasonable cause) the aldermen, capital burgesses; and freemen, shall choose another of the aldermen to be mayor, for the remainder of the year, he first taking the oath, which two or more aldermen are empowered to administer to him. And further our will is, that if any of the aldermen shall die or be displaced, (the which aldermen we will to be removable for a reasonable cause,) the mayor and common council to elect and appoint one of the capital burgesses to be an alderman, and shall take the usual oath. And it is our will, that if any of the capital burgesses shall die or be displaced, that others from among the freemen be chosen in their stead. Also it is our will that the said mayor, aldermen, and burgesses of the said borough, shall have a person of high repute and special eminence who shall he called high-steward (capitalis senescalis) of the borough, for the executing of all things belonging to the same office, by himself or his deputy, from time to time for ever, and that we constitute and make our beloved Thomas Savage, knight, and baronet, to be the first high-steward and after his decease, his son Sir John Savage, knight, to be high-steward during his life, and at their decease, the mayor, aldermen, and capital-burgesses, shall choose some eminent man to be high-steward, and each of these to take their oaths before the mayor of the said borough. And our will is, that an honest man to be the common clerk (communis clericus,) within the said borough, shall be chosen by the mayor and common-council, and also two serjeants at mace, the first of whom, to be called by his old name the catchpole, shall execute all writs, and processes, within the said borough, and shall be chosen by the mayor, aldermen, and burgesses, and the other shall he chosen by the mayor alone, shall be called the mayor's serjeant, and be the keeper of the gaol; and these two serjeants shall carry silver maces gilt before the mayor. And that the common clerk and mayor's serjeants shall be sworn before the mayor, and the catchpole before the steward. And our further will is, that the said Philip Oldfield, the mayor, and the aforesaid John Hobson, and Edward Drakeford, aldermen, shall be the first justices of the peace, of the said borough;

and that the mayor and two aldermen, to be chosen by the mayor, and capital-burgesses shall be the future justices; the said justices to keep the peace, and to keep and amend the weights and measures, and execute all other things which any justice of the peace for any single county, city, or corporate borough can do; yet so that they shall not in any wise, proceed to the trial of any treason, murder, felony, or such like matter touching the loss of life or limb, within the said borough. And that before they shall be admitted to the execution of the office of justice of peace, they shall take the requisite oaths; the said Philip Oldfield, before Sir John Brereton, knight, William Liversage, and William Swettenham, esqrs., and the said John Hobson, and Edward Drakeford, before the said Philip Oldfield; and the future mayor, and two aldermen when chosen to be justices, shall take the oaths before the last and next preceding mayor. And that the said mayor and justices may hold a general sessions of the peace, concerning all matters and things happening in the said borough, and execute all things therein as fully and completely as the justices of peace for any county, or borough, can do. And further of our ampler special grace and of our certain knowledge and pure affection, we grant that they may have a gaol for the safe keeping and imprisonment of all persons lawfully committed thereto; and the mayor's serjeant shall be the keeper of the same, he first giving security satisfactory to the mayor for the safe keeping thereof. And whereas Congleton is a parcel of the Duchy of Lancaster, and has three fairs yearly, and a weekly market on Saturday (in die sabbathi,) and a court leet, the incomes and profits of which make part of the revenues of the said Duchy. Yet our will is that, they may have another fair on Thursday before Shrovetide, and a court of pie-powder, with all the profits contingent to such fairs and courts, and the profits arising from the tolls, &c. of the said fair to the use of the said mayor, aldermen, and burgesses. And our further will is that if the mayor be sick, or absent for any reasonable cause, he may appoint another alderman to be deputy mayor, who shall have power to execute any thing even as if the mayor was present, he having first taken the oath before the mayor. And that the mayor and common clerk, shall have power to take recognizances and executions, according to the form of merchant's statute, and statute of Acton Burnel. And that the same mayor and clerk, shall have one seal of two parts, which seal shall he, and be called the king's seal, and of which the greater part shall be in the custody of the mayor, and the smaller part shall remain with the clerk; and that Roger Drakeford shall be the first clerk, during the pleasure of the mayor, aldermen and burgesses, and after the death or displacing of the said Roger Drakeford, the mayor, aldermen and burgesses, to choose another fit man to the office aforesaid, to be the clerk of us. Yet our will is, that the said Roger Drakeford and all others who shall succeed him, shall take an oath before the mayor for the faithful discharge of the office. And further we grant licence to the mayor, aldermen, and burgesses, to purchase and hold lands, tenements, and other hereditaments, not holden of us in capite[9], or by knight's service, to the yearly value of twenty pounds per annum, clear of reprisals. Also we grant leave to any of our subjects to sell or lease, such lands, tenements, &c. which are not held immediately of us. And we grant and confirm to the mayor, aldermen, and burgesses, of the said borough, all manner of customs, privileges, franchises, liberties, authorities, exemptions, acquittances, jurisdictions, roads, paths, markets, fairs, mills, services, messuages, lands, tenements, common of pasture, and hereditaments whatsoever, which were formerly granted to the town and its inhabitants, or officers, under different names, by any of the kings or queens of England, or by Henry de Lacy, or by any Earl of Chester, granted and confirmed; although some of them may not have been used, or have been misused, discontinued, or lost, and to have, and enjoy the same for ever, paying the accustomed fee-farm rents and services. And the mayor, aldermen and burgesses to have all liberties, franchises &c. hereby granted, without opposition from any of our justices, or servants; and they shall not be compelled to account for any abuse of their liberties committed before the date of this charter; and they shall have this charter, under the great seal of

England, without any fee being paid for the same to us in our hanaper, or elsewhere, for our use. That no express mention of the true yearly value of the premises, or of other gifts, and grants by us or any of our progenitors, made before these times to them, has been made in these presents, shall be no objection to their validity. In witness whereof, we have caused these our letters to be made patent. Witness ourself at Westminster, the 19th day of January, in the 22nd year of our reign over England, France, and Ireland, and the fifty eighth over Scotland. (i.e. January 19th, 1624,)

By writ of privy seal,

Yonge and Pye."

Charles the second, granted letters patent, to the burgesses. The first are dated March 10th, 1661, and the last March 14th, in the same year. These letters patent neither grant, nor allude to any further or greater privileges than those granted by Henry de Lacy; and although they are entitled on the back, "Exemplificatio Privilegiorum Burgi de Congleton," and were granted at the instance of the mayor, aldermen, and burgesses, yet they contain nothing that concerns them, except that it is said in two places, he claims so and so, "except of the free burgesses of Halton and Congleton."

The same king granted a charter to the burgesses, February 14th, 1666.—By the vast multiplicity of words employed in this charter, and the changes rung on privileges, franchises, liberties, &c. we might be led to suspect that it was a designed trick put upon the burgesses. It grants no new privileges, abridges some, and very cautiously confirms the remainder.

A memorandum, that freemen of Congleton are toll free at Chester, was determined at Chester, May 19th, 1564. — This memorandum is now of no effect, as the citizens of Chester do not claim tolls by grant or charter.

BYE-LAWS, &c.

In 1583, May 26th, at a court of orders.— That the viewers of the three wells, stockwell, the lower well, and the well at lawton-street end, shall appoint three or four neighbours to keep clean and sweet the said wells.

1584, Oct. 6th, ordered, — That every person of the counsel of this town, and is or hath been bailiff or catchpole, shall have of their own charges a gown or seemly black cloak, before the 1st of May, all which persons shall wear the same every fair day that the mayor shall walk the fair, on pain of forfeiting twenty shillings.

1590, At a court holden before William Llandin, deputy steward, three aldermen were sworn of the jury; and at the great court leet, 1601, five aldermen were sworn of the jury; from which it appears that the aldermen and capital burgesses may be called upon to serve on a court leet jury.

1637, Sept, 29th, ordered, — That four constables and five more of the freemen, not being of the common counsel, shall attend the mayor, to and from the chapel every Sunday and other holiday, and at other convenient times and places, as they shall be required, under the penalty of forfeiting five shillings.

Ordered at the same time,—That whatever person within this town, shall presume either by word or deed in an unseemly manner, to affront or abuse the mayor, deputy, or justices, constables, or other officers of this town, in the execution of his or their offices, shall, besides the legal penalty appointed in such cases, forfeit for every such offence, the sum of five shillings.

1671, May 19th, ordered, — That John Turner, ironmonger, shall be disfranchised from being any longer a freeman, by reason he seldom or never did give his appearance as other freemen usually doth, or to serve any office as other freemen have and doth do, &c. Also had notice given him this day to remove, by the four overseers and myself —No signature.

1757, May l0th, — Whereas of late, much more than in times past, divers inhabitants and tradesmen have made excuses to avoid being made freemen; and divers freemen have made excuses to avoid being made capital burgesses; and divers capital burgesses have made excuses to avoid being made aldermen; and divers aldermen have made excuses to avoid being made mayor or justices of the peace. It is therefore ordered, that every alderman who shall refuse to serve as mayor, when duly elected, shall forfeit the sum of five pounds; any alderman elected a justice, and in like manner refusing shall forfeit five pounds; any capital burgess elected an alderman and in like manner refusing, shall forfeit 13s. 4d. monthly, till he shall take upon himself the said office; any freemen elected a capital burgess, and in like manner refusing, shall forfeit 6s. 8d. monthly, till he shall take upon him the said office. In like manner that any inhabitant who shall be elected a capital burgess, and shall refuse to take upon himself the said office shall forfeit monthly 3s. 4d.

1789, August 26th, ordered, — That in future whenever the mayor shall attend to propose an alderman or capital burgess, at any meeting of this Assembly, he shall give three days notice (both inclusive,) to the members of this corporation, by the serjeant, of the name of such person as he proposes to move to be elected an alderman or capital burgess.

1805, Dec. 5th, ordered, — That the sweeping and cleaning of the streets, and the manure arising thereby, be let for one year in two divisions, the one from the middle of the town bridge eastwardly, and the other westwardly.—In another bye-law dated Sept. 15th, 1806, it was ordered, That if any other person, without leave from the person who has taken the same, shall sweep any of the streets between the channels or prevent the person appointed as aforesaid, he shall forfeit twenty shillings, to be recovered by action of debt.

At the same time, it was ordered, — That the constables (as formerly,) and also the crier of the court, wear cloaks (to be provided them) on all public occasions.

1806. Jan. 31st, Actions at law in the Court of King's Bench, were commenced against several persons who refused to take up their freedoms.

1815, Sep. 15th, ordered — That in future, every person coming to reside in this borough, and liable to purchase or take up his freedom, shall be compelled to purchase or take up the same immediately on coming to reside in the town.

1817, July 11th, ordered, — That if any person shall hereafter wheel any truck or wheelbarrow, upon any of the flagged or other footways within this borough, such person shall for every such offence, forfeit the sum of 2s. 6d.

1819, At an Assembly held Feb. 12th, the town-clerk stated that an application to the treasurer of the county, to be allowed out of the county rate, the expenses of prosecutors and witnesses, incurred in the prosecution of felons at the general quarter sessions of the peace for this borough, had been made and allowed.

THE OATH OF A FREEMAN.

You shall be faithful and true, and faith and truth shall bear to our Sovereign Lord King George, his heirs and successors. You shall be at the mayor's commandment for the time being in all things lawful. You shall obey all such laws, acts, and ordinances which from time to time shall be made and constituted by the body incorporate of this town. You shall well and truly yield and pay all and every such sum and sums of money from time to time which you shall be reasonably assessed or allotted to pay for the wealth and worship of this town. You shall not refuse any fitting office within this town, whereunto you shall be lawfully chosen. So help you God.

REFERENCES

1. *Lascy.* It is so in the original, and in all or most of the exemplifications, just at that place, though it is generally Lacy in other places, even of the same records.

2. *Guild merchant. (Gildam mercatoriam,)* A brotherhood of merchants or tradesmen, impowered to prohibit any person, who is not admitted of their society, from following any trade or traffic within the precincts granted to them, except at fairs.

3. *Pavage.* Money demanded for breaking the soil or pavement to drive posts into the ground, for erecting stalls more firmly. This seems to be the same as picage mentioned in other charters.

4. *Pontage.* Money demanded for leave to pass over a bridge.

5. *Lastage.* Toll paid for goods sold by the last, when placed in the open street or fair, as unpacked herrings, hides, wool, corn, rape seed, osmands, or iron stone.

6. *Murage.* Money demanded for passing through the gates of a walled city or place. The pretence for collecting this was for building and repairing the walls, in Latin Muros. Pontage and pavage demanded for the like reason.

7. *Approved or rented (approwyari et reddituari)* seems to mean, leave to enclose, improve, and fix the rent, as well as the renter, of the lands enclosed, without the interference of the usual approbatores, or Appruatores, (approvers,) who generally let such lands for the lords of the manor.

8. *A writ of right (breve de recto)* is a licence for a person ejected to sue for the possesion of an estate detained from him.

9. *In capite.* To hold of the king immediately, and not of any inferior lord who holds of the king.

Astbury and the Church

APPENDIX
ASTBURY CHURCH

This being the parish church under which the one at Congleton is a chapel of ease, and, consequently, closely connected with it in its history, claims a brief notice in this work. Of its original foundation we have no record, but that it is of considerable antiquity, is beyond doubt; for its existence at the time of the Conquest is recognized by Domesday[1]. About the year 1093, Gilbert Venables gave the church to the abbey of St. Werburgh at Chester, which grant is recited in the confirmation charter of that abbey by Hugh Lupus, in these words: "Likewise Gilbert de Venables gave to God and St. Werburgh, the church of Astbury, with a moiety of all the woods and lands (bosci et plani,) which belong thereto." The other moiety was afterwards granted by Sir William Venables to Hugh Venables, clerk, in the year 1188. It appears, from the records of the abbey, that Sir Roger Venables resumed the grant in 1259, and recovered possession of the advowson of Astbury, but, as recorded by the monks, his success was followed by a miserable death, within twelve months; and his son, Sir William Venables, again quit-claimed the church to the abbey[2].

The Norman barons of Cheshire, were equally tenacious with

the monks of St. Werburgh, and several generations after this grant, Henry, abbot of St. Werburgh, and Roger de Belgrave were summoned before Humphrey duke of Gloucester, then chief justice of Chester, to show why they opposed Sir Richard Venables in his right of presentation. In the year 1390, the cause was tried at Chester, and the right of the abbey was finally confirmed, and the advowson remained attached to it, until the dissolution of the monastery. After this dispute a licence was granted March 10, 1393, for the appropriation of the rectory and the endowment of a vicarage, but it was never acted upon.

The advowson of this valuable rectory was given by Henry the eighth to the dean and chapter of Chester, but this grant afterwards becoming void, it was given in fee-farm by Elizabeth to Sir Richard Cotton. In the division of these spoils it became the property of a zealous and much persecuted catholic Lady Egerton of Ridley, widow of Thomas Legh of Adlington. After passing through several families, it was purchased by the Crewe family, and is now the property of Lord Crewe.

The rector has all the tithes of the parish, which generally amount to about £2500. The præpositi or posts of the parish, nominate the church-wardens. The posts are the mayor of Congleton, and the proprietors of the halls of Brereton, Davenport, Eaton, Great Moreton, Little Moreton, Somerford, Radnor, and

Rode.

Among the records in the Tower, is a licence from Edward the first, during his wars with the Welsh in 1282, to John de Stanley, rector of Astbury, for buying provisions for the support of his household at St. Botolph's fair.

In the reign of Charles the first, there were a number of paintings and an organ in the church and the windows were chiefly composed of highly-finished painted glass, of which, during the civil wars, the greater part was demolished, and the organ, paintings and other relics of popish superstition, were removed into a field adjoining the burial-ground, and burned. They were destroyed in the year 1643, by a detachment of the parliamentary army, commanded by Sir William Brereton, when marching from Nantwich to Stafford castle. Sir William having heard that his nephew, Lord Brereton, had espoused the cause of the king, and had fled from Brereton hall to Biddulph hall, as a place of greater safety, he passed through Astbury in pursuing him thither, where, after a spirited resistance the latter was taken prisoner. From this period the church was closed, and continued in a dilapidated state until the restoration in 1660.

Considered as a building, this church which is dedicated to St. Michael, may vie with any in this or the neighbouring counties, in beauty and grandeur. It is a gothic structure, having a spire at its north-west angle; its interior consists of a nave, chancel and side aisles. There are five entrances and two porches, of which, one to the west is the same height as the middle aisle of the nave, and the other to the south the height of the side aisles.

The side aisles are separated from the nave by two rows of arches, five on each side, which are pointed and sprung from clustered pillars. The chancel is divided from the choir, at the end of the side aisles, by two corresponding arches; over these, is a row of clerestory windows in which are fragments of rich painted glass. The windows in the side aisles are pointed with quatrefoil heads; in the north chancel, there are windows of an earlier period, one of which being of the lancet Gothic form, and trefoil headed. The choir is separated from the body of the church, by carved Gothic screens, beautifully executed in oak; over the west screen is a rood loft, on which there was formerly an organ. It is surrounded by stalls of oak, ornamented with carving.

The roof is wholly of oak, tastefully carved and ornamented, where the beams intersect each other, with fanciful decorations; The present roof of the body of the church, appears to have been built in the years 1616 and 1617, as it bears those dates, and the name of "Richard Lownes, carpenter;" On the sides of the roof are the names and arms of the several prœpositi , or posts, at the time it was executed, namely, John Davenport, Philip Oldfield, William

Brereton, William Moreton, Randulph Rode, Edward Bellot, the mayor of Congleton, and William Leversage. Over the south end of the chancel is a rich pendant of carved oak, there is also another over the altar, with the hands and feet of our Saviour engraved at the bottom. The general design of the church is suited to a rich collegiate establishment, and the execution of the shrine-work, ancient carvings, and figures in the stained glass is exquisite.

The following are the principal inscriptions in the church:

In the nave are memorials of

Thomas Bowyer of Congleton, esq. obiit August 28, 1754.
And of Bridget his wife, obiit Feb. 28, 1784, aged 80.

A tablet, attached to a pillar on the north side is inscribed:

Near this place
lies interr'd the body of
George Lee,
of Eaton Hall, in this parish, esq.
who departed this life
the 4th April, 1773, aged 71 years.

Arms: Azure, 2 barrs Or, overall a bend compone, Or and Vert. Crest: on a wreath, a bear statant Sable, collared and chained Or.

At the east end of the north aisle is a private chancel, divided between the two manerial proprietors of Odd Rode. In the east window are the arms of Richard Blundeville earl of Chester. The steps of the altar still remain, with a closet for relics, and a piscina. — East of the altar steps is a large tomb bearing the memorials of

Dame Mary Jones,
died the 19th of April, 1743,
aged 85.
Sir William Moreton, knt.
recorder of the city of London,
died the 14th of March, 1763,
aged 67.
Dame Jane Moreton,
died the 10th of Feb. 1758,
aged 61.

At the other end of the chancel are the monuments of the Wilbrahams of Rode;. the first of which is attached to a pillar, with the arms of Wilbraham, inscribed:

Ricardus
Ranulphi Wilbraham, armr,
et Mariæ uxoris ejus
filius primogenitus,
antiqui stemmatis gerinen speciosum,
flos juvenum, patriæ spes, sui nominis decus,
sub ævi flore præreptus, hic jacet,
et terreni patrimonii factus exhæres,
cœlestem creavit hæreditatem
sexto die Feb. MDCCVI.
Sparge rosas, plecte corollas,
abi et fuge viator.

The following monuments are annexed to the north wall.

Near this place is buried Randle Wilbraham of Rode Hall, in the county palatine of Chester, esq. of which he was vice-chamberlain, also deputy steward of the university of Oxford, and barrister at law. He was second son of Randle Wilbraham of Townsend in Namptwich, in the same county, esq. by his wife Mary, daughter of Sir Richard Brooke of Norton, in the said county, bart. He died Dec. 3d, 1770, aged 76. His great industry and abilities carried him to the highest reputation and practice in his profession, which he adorned with sound knowledge, clear judgement, and steady integrity. He sate many years in parliament, where his publick conduct, superior to interest, or faction, shewed him a lover of his king and country, the laws and constitution of which he well understood and well maintained, loyal, upright, and independent. His private virtues shone in the husband, father, and friend, tender, careful, affectionate, candid, and easy. The natural goodness of his heart, he improved by sincere religion; he was a true Christian, and a firm member of the Church of England. He married Dorothea, daughter of Andrew Kenrick, esq. of Chester, barrister at law. She died Nov. 18th, 1754, aged 50, and was also interred here.

On the same tablet:
Ann Wilbraham, daughter of Randle and Dorothy,
died Dec. 5th, 1769, aged 39, and lies buried here.

Over the tablet is a sarcophagus, and over this, the arms of Wilbraham,
Argent, 3 bends Azure, a crescent of the second; impaling Kenrick, Ermine, a lion rampant Sable. Crest, on a wreath a wolf's head erased Argent.

On a tablet east of this monument:

Here lieth interred the body of Richard Wilbraham Bootle, esq. only son and heir of Randle Wilbraham, esq. of Rode Hall in this county, born Sept. 20th, 1725. He married May 31st, 1755, Mary, daughter and sole heiress of Robert Bootle, esquire, of Lathorn in the county of Lancaster, by whom he had six sons and eight daughters, of whom eight survived, namely, Edward, born March 7th, 1771, and Randle, born Jan. 10th, 1773; the daughters, Ann, married to Sir Richard Pepper Arden, master of the Rolls; Mary, to William Egerton, esq. of Tatton Park in this county; Francisca Alicia, to Anthony Eyre, esquire, of Grove, in Nottinghamshire; Sybilla Georgina, to William Farington, esquire, of Shaw Hall in Lancashire; Emma, to Charles Edmonstone, esquire barrister at law, London; Elizabeth unmarried. He was elected one of the representatives in parliament for the city of Chester at the accesion of his present majesty, October 1760, and served in five successive parliaments, where his conduct was uniform in support of his king and country, in the respectable character of an independent country gentlemen. He died March 13th, 1796, aged 71 years.

Arms. 1 and 4, Gules, on a chevron engrailed Argent, three crosses patée fitchée (intended for Bootle). 2 and 3, Azure, three bends wavy Argent, Wilbraham. An escutcheon of pretence, for Bootle.

The following inscription is on a neat tablet, west of the pyramidal monument.

This monument is erected
to the memory of
MARY,
wife of Richard Wilbraham Bootle, esq.
of Lathom House in Lancashire,
and Rode Hall in this parish;
she was born on the 17th of March, 1734,
and closed a life of exemplary usefulness,
benevolence and charity,
on the 10th of April, 1813,
in the 80th year of her age.

Near to the last is another tablet inscribed:
Sacred
to the memory of
Letitia, wife of
Randle Wilbraham, esq.
of Rode Hall,
who died on the 30th of March, 1805,
aged 27.
Sleep on, fair form, and wait th' Almighty's will,
Then rise unchang'd, and be an angel still.

There are several memorials in the south aisle of the Cartwrights of Smallwood, and of John Ford, of Eaton, gent. obiit Jan. 14, 1757, aged 78. Also, on a brass plate, an epitaph in memory of Christopher Byron, o f Buglawton, gent. died 5th of April 1674, aged 74.

Attached to the south wall are two marble tablets severally
inscribed:
Near this place
lies interred the body of
Edmund Swetenham, esq.
late of Somerford Booths,
in the county of Chester,
who departed this life
May the 7th, 1768.
in the 77th year of his age.

Also, of Susanna, relict of the said
Edmund Swetenham,
and daughter of Richard Wilmot,
late of Derby, in the county of Derby, M. D.
She died the l8th of May 1790, aged 77.

Near this place rest the mortal remains of Roger Swetenham esq. of
Somerford Booths in this county, whose life was distinguished by every
thing worthy of the man and the Christian; he was a most tender and
affectionate husband, a most kind and indulgent father, and a very sincere
and faithful friend. He died 27th of Jan. MDCCCIV, aged 55.

Also of Anne, relict of the said
Roger Swetenham,
who died July 12th, 1819, aged 56.

In the south angle of the chancel at the end of the south aisle, on an embattled altar-tomb, is a recumbent figure of a knight, armed in plate armour, with gorget of mail, and conical helmet; his surcoat is emblazoned with the arms of Davenport; the hands are clasped in prayer, and the feet rest on an animal.

On a slab, at the east end of this chancel is inscribed round the edges:

Hic jacet Amia Bellot de Grosvenour' familia oriunda, nuper Bellot de Moreton uxor, quæ obiit primo die Septembris a'no D'ni 1612.

Attached to the wall over this, is a shield of the arms of Bellot, impaling Grosvenor, with a crescent for difference.

On another slab:

Hic jacet Edw
ardus Bellot,
nuper de Moreto
n, ar. qui obiit VII
die Augusti an.
Dom'i 1622.

Over these are two marble mural monuments severally inscribed:

Hic requiescit in D'no Johannes Bellot de Moreton armig. qui cum laude patriæ et principi inservierat, postremos senectutis annos Deo consecravit, non pertæsus vitæ sed longe beatiorem anhelans de domo sua decressit et disposuit, et cum summo omnium (suorumq. præcipue) dolore excessit e vita nono die mensis Novembris an'o Domini 1659, ætat. suæ sexagessimo septimo. Habuit ex unica uxore sua filia et hærede Johan'is Bentley de Ashes in agro Staffordiæ gener novem liberos, quorum quatuor superstites reliquit.

Arms. Argent; on a chief Gules, three cinquefoils Argent, on a shield of pretence three bends wavy Sable for Bentley. Underneath, a shield emblazoned, quarterly, 1 and 4, Bellot; 2 and 3, Argent, on a head Sable three buckles Argent, Moreton.

M.S.

Subest quod relicquum Johan'is Bellot, baronetti, qui cum summa in Deum pietate, in egenos benignitate, in amicos humanitate, in omnes bonitate (ab inceptis nuptiis cum Anna filia Rogeri Wilbraham de Derfold, armig.) a'nos plus minus 25 fœlicifer egisset, hic juxta venerandi patris et charissimorum liberorum Johnnis et Annæ Bellot amatura morte præreptorum reliquias, suas etiam lubens deposuit, latam expectans resurrectionem; decimo quarto die mensis Julii a'no D'ni 1674. Hoc mortale i'mortalis amoris monumentum conjux mœstissima posuit.

Arms. Bellot. Wilbraham, Argent three bends wavy Azure.

In the north west angle of the chancel is a tomb inscribed:

T(homas) B(ellot)
was bured November the 10th,
anno D'ni 1654.
Mors mihi lucrum.

In the north-east angle is a marble monument inscribed :
Here lies the remains of
Peter Shakerley of Somerford Hall esq.
and likewise of Ann his first wife,
the daughter of John Amson of Lees
in the county of Chester, esq.
This tribute of filial affection

was erected by Eliza Buckworth,
their only surviving child,
to the memory of the
best of parents,
anno Dommin' 1796.

Over the above inscription is a sitting female figure, before an urn, over which hangs a weeping willow. Arms and crest of Shakerley, impaling Argent two barrs Argent, charged with three besants between leopards heads, cabossed Gules.

On a marble tablet adjoining are memorials of Dorothy Maria, infant daughter of C.W.J. Shakerley of Somerford, esq. by Dorothy his wife, obiit June 10, 1797: and of George Shakerley, infant son of the same, born April the 26th, died May 13th, 1802.

In the south-east angle of the chancel, is a female figure, habited in a close cap and ruff; over the figure are the arms of Grosvenor, with five quarterings. Round the edge of the tomb :
Hic jacet D. Maria Egerton, cx antiqua Grosvenorum familia oriuuda, nup'
Rio' Egerto' de Ridley equitis aurati uxor, plena annoru' xxv
At the end of the tomb:
Rodolphus Egerton de Ridley
maritus charissimus
in memoriam officiosæ pietatis
uxori bene merenti hoc
monumentum posuit
a D'ni 1609.

The following, on a slab before the altar-rails, is the only memorial of a rector, in the church.

Here lieth the body of the Reverend Tho. Rode,
Master of Arts, rector of this parish
near five years,
who departed this life the 26th day
of January, in the year 1731,
and in the 44th yeare of his age.

The following inscriptions are in the churchyard, the first of which is undoubtedly the most ancient.

Near the north-east angle of the church-yard, is a tomb over which is a raised pointed arch, with a pediment and pinnacles ornamented with crockets; within the arch at the west end is inscribed :

HIC JACENT RADULPHUS
BRERETON MILES ET DOMINA
ADA UXOR SUA, UNA FILIARUM DAVIDIS
COMITIS HUNT1NGDONIS[1].

On the tomb are two recumbent figures, an armed knight and his lady; on the north side of which, is the figure of an ecclesiastic resting on a slab, which forms the lid of a stone coffin, wholly above ground; on the south is the figure of an armed knight placed on an altar-tomb, the feet resting on an animal, the helmet conical, and the shield emblazoned two barrs, in chief three leopards' heads.

On a slab is the following inscription :

En lector
monumentum mortalitatis
saxea moles loco melioris
monumenti, sepulturam
indicans Joha'nis Latham
de Condate ter prætoris
cujus vita vere Christiana,
cujus mors amicis,
cognatis, præcipue luctuosa,
sibi jucunda, in
conspectu Dei proculdubio pretiosa.
Tam amanter,
quam hilarè, et
patienter, obiit 6° die
Feb. an'o salutis 1670,
ætatis suæ 62.

Near the north porch is a raised space inclosing four altar tombs,
two of which are inscribed :

Here lyeth interred
the body of William
Antrobus of Kent Green,
in Odd Rode,
who departed this life,

the first day of April,
Anno. Dom. 1688.
MORS MIHI LVCRVM.

Also

Margaret late wife of
the said William, was
buried Feb. ye 2. 1702.
Mary, daughter of Edmund and Ann Autrobus of Kent Green,
died April 17th, 1749, aged 77.
Philip Antrobus of Congleton, their son died June 3d, 1749,
aged 72.
Ann Antrobus, wife of Philip Antrobus,
died September 5th. 1775, aged 87.

On the two other tombs :

Here lieth the body of Philip
Antrobus of Congleton,
Gentleman, who died the 4th day
of November, 1788, aged 68.
Here also lieth the body of Mary Antrobus, wife of the said
Philip Antrobus, who died the
29th day of September, 1791,
aged 71.

Hannah Antrobus, died June 4th, 1772, aged 53.
John Antrobus of Congleton, gentleman, husband of the
said Hannah Antrobus, died Nov. 22d, 1773,

Mary Antrobus, died May 12th, 1802, aged 53.
Ann Antrobus, sister of the said John Antrobus, died May 12th
1807, aged 80.

The following inscriptions are on a slab and two altar tombs, near to
the south porch:

Here lyeth the body of
Elizabeth, the Wife of
William Lowndes of Smallwood,
that dyed ye 24 day of Avg.
Anno. Dom. 1690.
Also William Lowndes of Smallwood, dyed
October the 25th day, Anno Dom. 1716.

In memory of William Lowndes, gentleman, who died
the 3rd day of May, 1767, aged 79.
Also of Esther, his wife, who died Sept. 25th, 1729, aged 41.
And of Mary his second wife, who died Oct. 17th 1767, aged 78.

In memory of John Lowndes,
of Congleton, gentleman, he died
September 27th, 1792, aged 67.

Also of William Lowndes
formerly of Uttoxeter, late of Congleton, gentn.
Died 25th March, 1797, aged 54.

REFERENCES

1. Gilbert Venables holds Newbold Astbury, Ulvit did hold it. There is one hide and a half of land liable to pay taxes. There is a bookman, (or one that could read,) holds 100 acres, and the priest holds 100 acres. The whole is five carucates, (or 500 acres.) There are three villeins, and two borderers. There is a wood one mile long and one broad, and two enclosed pastures. In Edward the first's time Newbold Astbury was valued at twenty shillings, and the modus at eight shillings.

2. It will be necessary to inform the reader, that the information relating to this church is principally taken from Ormerod's History of Cheshire, and Lyson's Magna Britannia, Vol. 2. to which he is referred for the authorities there adduced.

3. This inscription is mentioned in church notes taken 1576, but is noticed as being in characters more modern than the rest of the monument, which in Camden's time was claimed by the families of Venables, Mainwaring, and Brereton. It is, however, presumed that the question is settled by the seal of the Venables of Astbury, which accords precisely with the arms on the shield of the figures. Ormerod.

THE END

The Lion & Swan Inn

King Charles the First Murthered.

Psal: 31. 13. for I have heard the slander of many, fear
was on every side, while they tooke Councill to
gether against me, they devised to take away
my life

Biographical Sketches
Of Eminent Men, Who Have Resided In
Congleton.

PRESIDENT BRADSHAW

When the biographer is employed in recording the actions of a man who was conspicuous in public life, in times when party spirit not only ran high, but the nation was actually engaged in a sanguinary civil war, the task is peculiarly difficult; because the writers on the side which he espoused blazoned forth his virtues in hyperbolical panegyric, while his adversaries stigmatized his name with every opprobrious epithet of obloquy and calumny. In this case nothing remains for the impartial narrator, but to collect his documents from the history of the age in which those calamitous transactions occurred, and from such private papers as bear the stamp of undoubted veracity; to give a perspicuous detail of plain matters of fact; and leave the reader to make his own conclusion. Such is the plan adopted in the following brief sketch of the life of John Bradshaw, a man of undoubted abilities, but whose reputation was blasted in consequence of his having been appointed by his compatriots to the unenviable office of judge of his former sovereign. It is, indeed, difficult for any man endowed with the common feelings of humanity, to read the account of the trial, condemnation, and decapitation of the unfortunate Charles, without strong emotions of regret; for, however censurable that king may have been in his unconstitutional exaction of part of the property of the people, he certainly was treated with great inhumanity by his implacable enemies the republicans. But the transactions of those days have long ceased to agitate the public mind; and it would be a most culpable negligence to omit in the present volume, the biography of a man, who, whatever were his merits or defects, was once exalted to the highest civic honours which the burgesses of Congleton could bestow; and afterwards stood so high in their estimation, as to be employed for many years as their principal law agent.

A branch of the family of Bradshaw, of Bradshaw, in Derbyshire, settled on a small estate in the township of Marple, near Stockport, about the middle of the sixteenth century. There John, the third son of Henry Bradshaw was born. The precise day of his birth is unknown, but he was baptized in the church of Stockport, as appears by the following memorandum in the parish register: "John the sonne of Henrye Bradshaw, of Marple, was baptized 10th Dec. 1602."

Of his juvenile habits, amusements, or disposition, little is known; but the places of his education are known by his will, where he mentions that he received the rudiments of classical learning at Bunbury in Cheshire, and was afterwards sent to the grammar school at Middleton, in Lancashire, which was then a seminary of high reputation. Tradition says that he was for some time a pupil in the grammar school at Macclesfield, where he evinced a propensity to poetical composition, and in imitation of some of the bards of antiquity, ever aspired to a combination of the character of poet and prophet, of which the following lines remain a proof:

> My brother Henry must heir the land;
> My brother Frank, must be at his command;
> Whilst I, poor Jack, will do that,
> Which all the world shall wonder at.

Whether these lines were really the offspring of our young statesman's juvenile muse, or the production of some other inventive genius, is of little consequence; but they were literally verified; for the hereditary estate descended to John Bradshaw's eldest brother, and he was left to make his way in the world by the exertion of his strong natural abilities.

That he was a youth of promising parts is evident from the fact, that after he had received a competent education, he was bound apprentice to an attorney in Congleton, and at the expiration of his apprenticeship, was sent by his father, to finish his studies in the law at Gray's Inn, London. There he formed some of those early connexions with his fellow-students which promoted his future advancement in life. He was soon afterwards called to the bar, and returned to Congleton. He went the regular circuit with the judges, as councellor at law for some years, and obtained considerable influence in Congleton, his favourite place of residence at this period of his life. From a memorandum in the corporation books, it appears that in the year 1637, John Bradshaw was elected mayor. He was a vigilent and intelligent magistrate, and perfectly qualified by his knowledge of the common law of the land to administer justice. During his mayoralty several bye-laws were made by the corporation for the better government of the town.

There are no memorials of his private life, or public character from the year 1637, till 1646; and it seems to have been the intention of the historians who wrote after the restoration, to hold up his name to the detestation of the friends of royalty, and to cast his descendants into the deepest oblivion. It is not therefore, well ascertained whether he was married or left any issue.

As a public man, he first came into notice in the year 1646, when the parliament appointed him one of the three commissioners of the great seal for six months. He performed the duties of this office so much to the satisfaction of his employers, that in February, 1647, he was raised to the honorable office of chief justice of

Chester, and also appointed one of the judges of Wales, by the unanimous vote of both houses of parliament.

But the moment was fast approaching in which he was called to that unenviable preeminence which cast a shade over his character both as a statesman and a man. On the 3d of January, 1648 the lords adjourned, having first by a resolution entered on their journal, rejected the ordinance passed by the house of commons for the trial of the king. The commons immediately took the whole responsibility of the business upon themselves; passed an act for the appointment of a high court of justice for the trial of the deposed and imprisoned king.

On the 10th of January, when the commissioners met, they nominated Sergeant Bradshaw for their President. He was absent at the time, and officiating as a judge at guild-hall, London; but on being informed of his appointment, he chose a deputy to act as judge in his place, and undertook the solemn task of presiding at the court. The event of that trial is recorded in history; the unfortunate and magnanimous Charles was beheaded before his own palace, at Whitehall on the 30th of January; and died with the calmness of a philosopher and the serenity of a christian. After the fall of Charles, the republicans, of whom President Bradshaw was undoubtedly the most ardent and resolute, enjoyed a temporary triumph, till they were awakened from their illusory dream of independence, by military despotism of Oliver Cromwell.

The parliament, apprehensive of the increasing influence of that successful general, passed an act on the 14th of February, 1648, for the nomination of a council of state. It consisted of thirty-eight members, some of whom were men of distinguished abilities, and among that number was President Bradshaw. The parliament were not unmindful of his public services, and the promptitude and decision which he evinced in their cause, for in June, 1649, the sum of £1000 was voted to him; and soon afterwards an annuity of £2000, was settled upon him by the unanimous vote of the house.

When Cromwell dissolved the long parliament, as it was called; he did not think the revolution complete till he had also deposed the council of state. He, therefore, proceeded boldly to the room where they sat, with President Bradshaw in the chair, and thus addressed them; "If you, gentlemen, are met here as private persons, you shall not be disturbed; but if as a council of state, this is no place for you, since you cannot but know what was done in the house in the morning, so take notice that the parliament is dissolved." To this address, Bradshaw, with his characteristic intrepidity, replied; "Sir, we have heard what you did in the house in the morning, and before many hours all England will hear it. But Sir, you are mistaken in thinking parliament is dissolved; for no power under heaven can dissolve them, but themselves; therefore, take you notice of that." But the courage and animation of Bradshaw were unavailing upon this occasion; for Cromwell confiding in the attachment of the army, perseveringly carried his point; effected a new revolution in the government, and assumed the title of Lord Protector.

The spirited opposition of Bradshaw to the usurper's ambitious project was not forgotten by him, although he affected to treat the President with respect; and he acknowledged to a confidential friend, that he did not think his work complete, even after the dissolution of the long parliament, till he had also dissolved the council of state, and "this I did," says he, "in spite of the objection of honest Bradshaw the President."

But Cromwell was too acute a politician to suffer men of known abilities to remain unemployed; accordingly he summoned Bradshaw, and others whom he knew were inimical to his usurpation, but might, nevertheless, be made useful to the state, to the council convened by him for the government of the commonwealth. When the Protector saw Bradshaw at the council, he required him to take out a new commission for his office of chief justice of Chester, under the authority of the Protectorate, which he refused to do, alledging that he held that place by a grant from the parliament of England, and whether he had performed the duties of his office with integrity, he was willing to submit to the decision of a jury of twelve Englishmen, to be chosen even by Cromwell himself. This firmness seems to have overawed the usurper, for Bradshaw was suffered to go his circuit as chief justice of Chester without interruption.

That President Bradshaw was popular in his native county, is evident from the fact, that in the year 1654, he was returned as representative in parliament for Cheshire. As a senator he was the steady champion of what he considered constitutional liberty, and so strenuously opposed the ambition of Cromwell, that it was thought necessary to have recourse to state intrigue to prevent his being returned a second time.

After the demise of Cromwell, President Bradshaw was again returned for Cheshire, to the parliament which met in January, 1658, and was nominated by the house one of the commissioners to hold the broad seal for five months. He was soon afterwards deprived of this office by the army which ushered in the restoration. But he died in the year 1659, before that event took place. On the 30th January, 1661, his body was taken out of the grave by an order of government, and drawn on a sledge to Tyburn, where it was suspended on the gallows, with the remains of Cromwell, and Ireton.

By President Bradshaw's will, which is dated March 22d, 1653, it appears that he was possessed of considerable lauded property, and that he made many charitable bequests. But on the restoration, the whole property which had been his, was confiscated to the crown.

JOHN WHITEHURST, F. R. S.

JOHN WHITEHURST[1], whose philosophical and mechanical researches have been justly held in such high estimation, was born at Congleton, April, 10th, 1713; and was the son of John Whitehurst, clock and watch maker in this town. Of the early part of his life little is known; on his quiting school, where the education he received was certainly very defective, he was bred up by his father to his own business; in which, as in other mechanical and scientific pursuits, he soon gave intimations of future eminence.

At about the age of twenty-one, his eagerness after new ideas carried him to Dublin, having heard of an ingenious piece of mechanism in that city, consisting of a clock with certain curious appendages, which he was extremely desirous to see, and also to converse with the maker. On his arrival, however, he could neither procure a sight of the former, nor draw the least hint from the latter respecting it. Thus disappointed he thought of an expedient for the accomplishing of his design; and accordingly took up his residence in the house of the mechanic, paying liberally for his board, as he had hopes from thence to obtain the indulgence wished for. He was accommodated with a room adjoining the one in which the favourite piece of mechanism was kept. He had not long to wait to satisfy his curiosity, for, the artist being one day employed in examining his machine, was suddenly called down stairs; which the young enquirer happening to overhear, went softly into the room, inspected the machine, and having discovered the secret, escaped unobserved to his own apartment. His end thus compassed; he soon afterwards returned to Congleton.

It was prior to this period, that, from his vicinity to the many stupendous phenomena in Derbyshire, constantly presented to his observation, his attention was excited to inquire into their origin and causes. His father, who was a man of an inquisitive turn, encouraged him in every thing that tended to enlarge the sphere of his knowledge, and occasionally accompanied him in his subterraneous researches.

About the year 1747, he left Congleton, and commenced business at Derby, where he made the clock at the town-hall, in order to his being enrolled a burgess; the clock and chimes in the beautiful tower of All-saints church were also executed by him. On January 9th, 1747, he married Elizabeth, daughter of the reverend George Gretton, rector of Trusley, in Derbyshire. Her talents and education were very respectable, which enabled her to be useful in correcting some parts of his writings.

Being appointed stamper of the money weights, when the act passed in 1775, for the regulation of the gold coin, through the recommendation of the Duke of Newcastle, he removed to London. While resident in the country, strictly attentive to his own immediate and very extensive business, he had been consulted in almost all the undertakings in Derbyshire, and the neighbouring counties, where the aid of superior skill in mechanics, pneumatics, and hydraulics, was requisite; and on his settling in town, his house became the resort of the ingenious and scientific at large, and this to such a degree as frequently to impede him in the prosecution of his own speculations.

In the year 1778, he published his "Enquiry into the Original State and Formation of the Earth" of which a second edition appeared in 1786, considerably enlarged and improved. He was elected and admitted a fellow of the royal society, May 13th, 1779; he was also member of some other philosophical societies, which admitted him of their respective bodies without his previous knowledge. Before he was admitted a member, three several papers of his had been inserted in the Philosophical Transactions, namely, Thermometrical Observations at Derby, vol. 57, no. 28. An account of a Machine for raising Water, at Oulton in Cheshire, vol. 65, no. 24: and Experiments on Ignited Substances, vol. 66, no. 38.

In the summer of 1783, he made a second visit to Ireland, with a view to examine the Giant's Causeway and other northern parts of that island, which he found composed of volcanic matter; an account of which were given in the second edition of his "Inquiry." During this excursion, he erected an engine for raising water from a well, to the summit of a hill, in a bleaching ground, at Tullidoi, in the county of Tyrone; it is worked by a current of water, and for its utility, perhaps, unequalled in any country.

In the year 1787, he published "An attempt towards obtaining invariable Measures of Length, Capacity, and Weight, from the Mensuration of Time." His plan is, to obtain a measure of the greatest length that conveniency will permit from two pendulums whose vibrations are in the ratio of 2 to 1, and whose lengths coincide with the English standard in whole numbers. The numbers he has chosen shew great ingenuity. On a supposition that the length of a seconds pendulum, in the latitude of London, is 39.2 inches, the length of one vibrating 42 times in a minute, must be 80 inches; and of another vibrating 84 times in a minute, must be 20 inches; and their difference 60 inches, or five feet, is his standard measure. The apparatus, by which the difference of the pendulums was ascertained, is of curious construction, and deserves notice; it consists of a spherical leaden ball, two inches in diameter, weighing 25 oz. 10 dwt. 11 gr. troy, suspended by a flat, tempered, steel wire,

80 inches of which weigh only three grains, the extreme fineness of this wire almost passes credibility. Its length and breadth are not given; but by calculation, 80 inches in length weighing three grains, and the specific gravity of tempered steel being 7.704, its thickness, were it a square rod, would be only the 228th part of an inch. It, nevertheless, supports above 2lb. of lead; which is a surprising instance of the attraction of cohesion.

Although Mr. Whitehurst had for some years felt himself gradually declining, yet his ever active mind remitted not of its accustomed exertions; even in his last illness, before being intirely confined to his room, he was proceeding at intervals to complete a treatise on chimnies, ventilation, and garden stoves, announced to the public in 1782.

He was at times subject to slight attacks of the gout, and on the 5th of December, 1787, after incautiously exposing himself to cold, he had a sudden attack of that disease in his stomach. This complaint soon became serious; and his illness was long and painful. He was removed to a friend's house at Chelsea, for the benefit of the air; where he made but a short stay, for, not finding the advantage which was expected, he was desirous to be removed back to his own house. After his return his strength began to fail more rapidly, by a strong febrile paroxysm which now commenced; he was sensible of approaching dissolution; he met it with perfect resignation; and, on

February 18th, 1788, in the 75th year of his age, terminated his laborious and useful life.

However respectable Mr. Whitehurst may have been in mechanics, and those other parts of natural science which he more immediately cultivated, he was of far higher account with his acquaintance and friends on the score of his moral qualities. To say nothing of the uprightness and punctuality of his dealings in all transactions, relative to business; few men have been known to possess more benevolent affections than he, or, being possessed of such, to direct them more judiciously to their proper ends. Though well known to many of the great, to whose good graces flattery has been found in general the readiest path, it is to be recorded to his honor, that he never once stooped to that degrading mode of obtaining favor, which he regarded as the lowest vice of the lowest mind. He had indeed a settled abhorrence, not of flattery only, but of every other deviation from truth, at whose shrine he may be said to have been a constant worshipper. The truth of things he was daily more or less employed in investigating, and truth of action he exemplified in the whole tenor of a long and singularly useful life.

REFERENCES

1. This brief sketch of John Whitehurst, is extracted from 'Authentic Memoirs of his Life and Writings' published in the Universal Magazine

S. Yates, Printer,
Congleton

Additional Appendices
A Letter from John Bradshaw of Grey's Inn to
Sir Peter Legh of Lyme.

Edited by Wm. Langton Esq.
Extracted from
"Remains Historical & Literary
Connected with the Palatine Counties of Lancaster and Chester"
Published by The Chetham Society 1856

INTRODUCTION

The following letter was found among the muniments at Lyme. It is written on one page of a sheet of foolscap paper in a small neat hand, of which the signature is a fair example. The letter, interesting in itself as an illustration of the times, becomes the more so when we consider the great probability of its being the youthful production of a man, whose character and career were alike remarkable.

If it be objected that the subscription of the letter, given here in facsimile, bears no close resemblance to the firm and free writing of the same name affixed to the death warrant of King Charles, it may fairly on the other hand be urged, that the signature acquired by most men in official routine differs materially from the familiar writing of their youth, and possesses a character and boldness beyond that of their ordinary text. Another element of doubt must also be mentioned. There were two John Bradshawes contemporaries at Gray's Inn, the one admitted a student in 1620, the other in 1622; and, the original archives of that house having perished, it is not possible to determine with absolute certainty which of these was the future President of the High Court of Justice, or which was the writer of this letter.

Though it does not bear a complete date, the letter contains internal evidence of having been penned on the 13th of June, 1623. The style is not unlike that of the President, while the orthography is also similar in character to his; but the circumstance, which yields the strongest presumption of its having been an early production of the stern old republican, lies in the appeal made to Sir Peter Legh, as the influential neighbour of the writer's father.

John Bradshawe "the Regicide" was the third son of Henry Bradshawe of Marple Hall, an estate lying in close proximity to that of the great family of Legh at Lyme. Born in 1602, and baptised at Stockport on the 18th December of the same year, he must have been nearly twenty-one years of age when this letter was written. It is stated by his biographers that he had served a clerkship in the office of an attorney at Congleton, before he entered himself as a student for the bar at Gray's Inn.

Milton, his friend, says of him: Est Joannes Bradscianus nobili familia, ut satis notum est, ortus; unde patriis legibus addiscendis, primam omnem ætatem sedulò impendit; dein consultissimus causarum ac disertissimus patronus, libertatis et populi vindex acerrimus, et magnis reipublicæ negotiis est adhibitus, et incorrupti judicis munere aliquoties perfunctus; tandem uti regis judicio præsidere vellet, à senatu rogatus, provinciam sane periculosissimam non recusavit. Attulerat enim ad legum scientiam ingenium liberale, animum excelsum, mores integros ac nemini obnoxios;

He appears to have been first employed by the Government in 1644; and, once embarked in public life, the history of his career continues interwoven with the annals of his country. After his decease in 1659, his remains were deposited in Westminster Abbey; and at the restoration of King Charles the Second they were removed to Tyburn and gibbeted.

Viewed through the disturbing medium of political strife, no one has been characterized by more widely contrasting epithets than John Bradshawe; but men of all parties must be struck with his extraordinary firmness, his singleness of purpose, and his courage. He never faltered while sitting in judgment on the King, nor ever repented of that deed: and, when in the arbitrary exercise of power Cromwell had dissolved the Parliament and dismissed the Council of State, he met the Usurper with stern rebuke and defiance. **W. L.**

LETTER FROM JOHN BRADSHAWE

Worthy S^{ur}

    I receyved yor Answer to my last l͠re by yor servant
Birchenhalgh, ffor which I humblie thanke you, assuring my self
thereby of yor continued ffavor in theise my troublesome stormes,
towards me so meane & unworthy of the least exp^rssion of yor
Love. But for all this yor goodnes, I shall pmyse you this payment,
to wryte it wth a pen of brasse in the tables of my heart, wch can as
yet resound onelie prayse and thanksgyving. Concerning my l͠re to
my ffather I will onelie say thus much, It had too much Reason on
my syde, for so impartiall a Justice as he knew yor self was to see
& arbitrate my cause, ffor the ballance of neutralitie wherein he
supposed he held you, would questionles on his part be y^rby ov^r-
turned. But let him do what he please, he shall soon^r be wearie of
aflicting, then I will be of suffering, & by the grace of God I will
shew my self a Sonne, though he cease to be my ffather. But to
end this unpleasing argum^t, I will onelie in conclusion ppound this
one Dilemma unto yor noble Construction — What ffruit that ffath^r
may expect to come of his sonnes studyes, that wittinglie doth sup-
presse the instrument of his labors, & willinglie keepe in ffetters
the freedome of his mynd, wch is that chosen toole appoynted for the
fynishing of all such high attempts, & whether the worke, imperfect by reason of such Restraynt, be layd to his charge that assumed
it, or to him that was the Impediment, and yet was bound to have

helped the Accomplishing of the Enterpryse. I know S^r you understand & by this short question, you may gesse what may furth^r
be urged, but I leave all to yor judgm^t and reposing my self on yor
worth, I feare no disastrous censure.

ffor neglecting the Exercyses of the howse, it is a fryvolous objection, Himself hath been satysfyed in it and Mr. Damport will justify
me, knowing I never neglected but one Exercyse of myne owne, w^{ch}
was to argue a case, wch according unto course another should have
done for me at my first coming to the howse, & I by ffeeing the
Butler did of purpose neglect it, onelie deferring the tyme, that after
I had been heere a whyle, I might pleade the case for myself; w^{ch}
is so far from a fault, that contrarywyse the best students have
ever taken this course, & is & hath been comended of those that
understand it, & hereof I very well know my ffath^r can not be
ignorant, having been acquaynted therewth. But it seemeth, how
prone he is, to take exceptions agaynst me, when fynding nothing
blameworthy, he returnes that for a fault, wch deserveth allowance
and prayse. Concerning Mr. Damport, he is a worthy Gentleman,
his Love to me doth cause me to respect him & his worth, in
honestie to regard him. But I thanke you for yor noble advyse,
& should esteeme my self base not to pursue and follow it, still
wayting a good howre, when God shall be pleased to enable me to
gyve lyfe unto my words by deeds equyvalent thereto. In the
meane tyme, the trybute of a thankfull heart I pay you.

Ffor o^r domestique newes, I have sent you the Cause of my Lo: of
Oxford wch is to be heard this Terme. The plot it is thought hath
been to terryfie him so from his Offyce, as to yeld his place of High
Chamberleyn of England to the high swolne ffavoryte and his
famylie, wch his great heart will never yeld to; & therefore to
make him, if not depending, beholding to his greatest Enemie, it is
lykelie, for his words he shall be shrewdlie censured, & so remayne
in Durance, till Buckingham returne from Spayne and gratify him
wth his libertie & a release of his ffyne & so asswage his stomacke by
this his plotted good turne. As it succeeds, I will certyfie you.
The Ships are yet on the Downes, having been crossed & kept

backt by contrary wynds from their voyage. We heare no newes from Spayne, nor have not heard, this month, onlie as it is suspected, the Princes Entertaynm^t continues not so gloryous as it hath been. It is hitherto a true observation, that England hath been ffatall to Dukes, but above all most omynous unto the Dukes of Buckingham, of wch the Marquesse hath the tytle, & lykewyse Earle of Coventrie, & the Duke of Lenox is created Duke of Rich-mond & Earle of Newcastle upon Tyne, & more Dukes & Earles are expected to hono^r this liberall Age. Kit Villers is made Earle of Anglesey in recompense of Barkshyres escape, & to increase the kindred, hath marryed wth Shelton, his moth^{rs} sisters daughter; but we are so used to wonders, that this is none at all. Lenox Arundell Pembroake & some other Nobles, who are styled the Lords of the Receptions,˙ have been at Southampton & Ports-mouth to p^{r}pare royall lodgings & entertaynm^t, for the Prince & his Bryde of Spayne, whensoever they arryve.

Ffor o^r forreyn newes I have sent you all we have had any tyme this month, amongst wch I have sent you the parliam^t of Regens-purgh, holden by the Emperor and his Princes, wherein you may see what is done for the disposing of the Electorship of the forlorne Palatyne, a discourse not unworthy yor knowledge, who I am sure are as zealous for the good of the countrey & ffriends as those that beare greater sway & have better power of performance, be they but subjects of England. To conclude all my relatyons I will tell you of one mad prancke that happened wthin theise two nights. Sr Thomas Bartley was arrested hard by Grayes Inne for 4000^{ls} debt, & was carryed to the higher end of Holborne, and comitted under custody: About 12 of the clocke at night some Gentlemen of o^r howse and of Lincolnes Inne, met togeth^r for his Rescue, broke downe the howse, tooke him away wth them, beat the Constables Serjeants & Watchmen, & though St Gyles was raysed & almost all Holborne, yet they with their swords & pistolls kept them of, & brought him along to Grayes Inne: there were dyvers hurt wth Halberds, & about 200 swords drawne, & at least 2000 people. There are 5 or 6 Gent. taken & sent to Newgate, & wee heare that the Names of above 60 Gent: are gyven up to the King; what will be done about it, we shall know in tyme. There are more murthers drownings deaths & villaynies, then hath been knowne in London of long tyme before. I had almost forgot the Moderator a booke uncerteyn weth^r wrytten by a papist or a statesman (for indeed they are now so linked, as scarce can admit distinguishm^t) for p^rparing a way to reconciliation, between the Papists and us; howsoev^r by whomsoev^r, or to what end soev^r it is penned, it is a treatise I am sure, excellently curyous and cautelous and may stand o^r syde in much stedd when they please to make use of it.

I will now drawe to an end, intreating yor wo^p not to miscensure my forwardnes in takyng notyce of theise things, for it agrees wth my genius to have some smattering herein, neyther do they any whyt hinder, but further my studyes and judgm^t.

And so wth most humble thanks for all yor wo^{ps} favo^{rs}, I remayne yor debtor for them, beseeching God Almightie to p^rserve and psper you for the good of many, & my most specy^{ll} comfort

ever resting

yor wo^{ps} to dispose

Grayes Inne the
First day of the
Terme.

Jo: 2Bradshawe

To the Right Wor^{pll} Sr Peter
Legh Knight att Lyme in
Cheshyre.

1818

STOCKPORT

ALTRINGHAM

Hayfield

CHAPEL
en le Frith

KNUTSFORD

MACCLESFIELD

CONGLETON

SANDBACH

...ORDSHIRE

1830

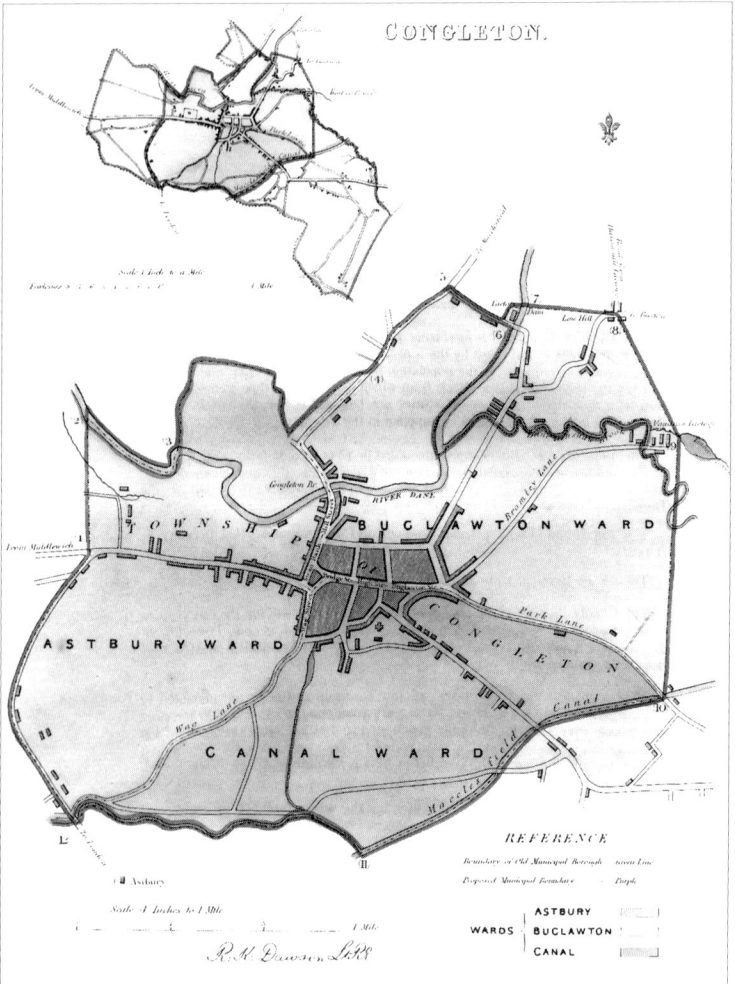

CONGLETON.

Scale 4 Inch to a Mile

T O W N S H I P

BUGLAWTON WARD

ASTBURY WARD

CANAL WARD

CONGLETON

RIVER DANE

Park Lane

Wag Lane

Macclesfield Canal

REFERENCE

| Boundary of Old Municipal Borough | .... | Screen Line |
| Proposed Municipal Boundary | . . . . | Parish |

WARDS
| ASTBURY |
| BUGLAWTON |
| CANAL |

Scale 4 Inches to 1 Mile

R.K. Dawson Lithg.

1835

C O N G L E T O N.

REPORT upon the Proposed Municipal Boundary and Division into Wards of the Borough of Congleton.

THE Borough of Congleton ·is co-extensive with the Township of Congleton, Ancient Limits which is one of several constituting the Parish of Astbury. The Boundaries are of the Borough. well defined, and an accurate plan of the Borough on a large scale, made in 1795, is in the possession of the Corporation ; we forward a copy of this Plan on a reduced scale, with such alterations as the increase of population and the changes of circumstances in the Town have made necessary.

The Town of Congleton is increasing rapidly in every direction. The impulse Trade and Manu- given to the trade of this place by the repeal of the Duties on French Silks, caused factures. an increase of 50 per cent. in the population between 1821 and 1831, and although in 1825 the trade received a shock from which it took some time to recover, it is now in a flourishing state ; new factories are building, and at present there is a demand for labour which cannot be supplied in the Town.

The Population of the Borough amounted in 1831 to 9,352, the principal part Population. of this number is congregated in the Town of Congleton and its immediate vicinity, not more than 400 being distributed throughout the agricultural portion of the Borough.

The Population of the present Borough of Congleton amounted in 1831 to Population of 9,352. present Borough.

There is no Borough Rate levied for any purpose. Borough Rate.

The County Rate in the Borough of Congleton amounted for the last year to County Rate. 320 *l.*, equivalent to a Rate of 6 *d.* in the pound ; while in the Township of Buglawton it amounted for the same period to 131 *l.* 13 *s.*, equivalent to a Rate of 8 *d.* in the pound.

The Poor Rate for the last year in the Township of Congleton amounted to Poor Rate. 1,860 *l.* ; this was raised by twelve Rates, each amounting to 155 *l.*, and in assessing this, houses were rated at 3 *d.* in the pound, and land at 4 *d.*, upon two-thirds of the actual value ; in Buglawton in the same period 12 levies were made, each amounting to 42 *l.* 1 *s.* 5 *d.*, and the land was rated at 3 *d.*, and buildings at 2 *d.* in the pound, upon two-thirds of the rental.

The Town is paved by the Corporation, but the streets are not generally in a Paving. good state of repair.

The Town is well lighted with Gas at an expense of about 200 *l.* per annum, Lighting. which is defrayed by a Rate under the provisions of the Act 3 & 4 Gul. IV. c. 90.

To the North of the Town the Boundary, which on that side runs down Daven- Circumstances shaw Brook, approaches within a few hundred yards of the extreme Limit of the considered in pro- Town of Congleton. On the other side of the Brook, in the Township of Buglawton, posing a Boundary. several factories have been built, and a large Population has congregated round them, and there is every prospect in a few years of this suburb being joined to the Town by a continuous street ; we therefore think it advisable to include within the Borough that portion of the Township of Buglawton, comprised in the angle, between the Brook and the River Daven, and to propose the following Boundary as the best which under the present circumstances we could adopt :—

PROPOSED
BOUNDARY.

From the Point (1) at which the Middlewich Road leaves the London Road, in a straight Line due North to the Point at which such straight Line cuts the River Daven (2); thence, Eastward, along the River Daven to the Point (3) at which the same leaves the Boundary of the Old Borough; thence, Northward, along the Boundary of the Old Borough to the Point (4) at which the same meets the Macclesfield Road; thence, Northward, along the Macclesfield Road to the Northernmost Point (5) at which the same meets the Boundary of the Old Borough; thence, Eastward, along the Boundary of the Old Borough to the Point (6) at which the same meets the Western Boundary Wall of a Factory on the Western Side of the River Daven; thence, Northward, along the Boundary Wall of the said Factory (including the Factory within the Borough) to the Dam of the said Factory (7) on the River Daven; thence in a straight Line to the Point (8) at which the Road from Congleton to the Havannah Factory leaves the Buxton Road; thence in a straight Line to the Dam (9) of Mr. Vaudrie's Factory on Timber Brook; thence in a straight Line to the Point (10) at which Park Lane crosses the Macclesfield Canal; thence, Westward, along the Macclesfield Canal to the Point (11) at which the same crosses the Boundary of the Old Borough; thence, Westward, along the Boundary of the Old Borough to the Point (12) at which the same crosses the London Road; thence, Northward, along the London Road to the Point first described.

The Population within these limits will amount to 10,500.

WARDS.

The following Division into Three Wards coincides with that which has been adopted by the Revising Barristers for the ancient Borough; and the addition of that portion of the Township of Buglawtown included within the proposed Boundary to No. 2 Ward, will not constitute such an inequality between the Wards as to render any alteration necessary.

Boundary of
Ward No. 1, or
Astbury Ward.

Ward No. 1, or *Astbury Ward:*

From the Point at which the Macclesfield Road meets the Boundary of the Borough, Southward, along the Macclesfield Road to the Point at which the same meets Mill Street; thence along Mill Street to the Point at which the same meets Swan Bank; thence along Swan Bank to the Point at which the same meets Wag Street; thence along Wag Street to the Point at which the same meets Wag Lane; thence along Wag Lane to the Point at which the same crosses the London Road; thence Southward, along the London Road to the Point at which the same meets the Boundary of the Borough; thence, Westward, along the Boundary of the Borough to the Point first described.

Boundary of
Ward No. 2, or
Buglawton Ward.

Ward No. 2, or *Buglawton Ward:*

From the Point at which the Macclesfield Road meets the Boundary of the Borough, Southward, along the Macclesfield Road to the Point at which the same meets Mill Street; thence along Mill Street to the Point at which the same meets Swan Bank; thence along Swan Bank to the Point at which the same meets Duck Street; thence along Duck Street to the Point at which the same meets Bridge Street; thence along Bridge Street to the Point at which the same meets High Street; thence along High Street to the Point at which the same meets Buglawton Street; thence along Buglawton Street to the Point at which the same meets Park Lane; thence along Park Lane to the Point at which the same meets the Boundary of the Borough; thence, Northward, along the Boundary of the Borough to the Point first described.

Boundary of
Ward No. 3, or
Canal Ward.

Ward No. 3, or *Canal Ward:*

From the Point at which the London Road crosses the Boundary of the Borough, Northward, along the London Road to the Point at which the same meets Wag Lane; thence along Wag Lane to the Point at which the same meets Wag Street; thence along Wag Street to the Point at which the same meets Swan Bank; thence along Swan Bank to the Point at which the same meets Duck Street; thence along Duck Street to the Point at which the same meets Bridge Street; thence along Bridge Street to the Point at which the same meets High Street; thence along High Street to the Point at which the same meets Buglawton Street; thence along Buglawton Street to the Point at which the same meets Park Lane; thence along Park Lane to the Point at which the same crosses the Boundary of the Borough; thence, Westward, along the Boundary of the Borough to the Point first described.

RETURN.—Corporation of CONGLETON, Parish of Astbury, County of Chester.

	1835.
	NUMBER of Persons rated for Houses, Warehouses, Shops, and Counting-houses, and who were not excused on account of Poverty.
In present Borough - - - -	1,789
In proposed Borough - - - -	1,867
	Of these, what Number Householders :
In present Borough - - - -	1,785
In proposed Borough - - - -	1,863

J. Hammill.

W. Denison.

BOROUGH OF CONGLETON.

NAMES OF STREETS.	Sides of Street.	Number of Inhabited Houses on each side of Street.	Amount of Assessment on each Side of Street.	Rate Payers, divided into Six Classes, as below: At and under £. 5.	Above £. 5, up to £. 10.	Above £. 10, up to £. 20.	Above £. 20, up to £. 30.	Above £. 30, up to £. 40.	Above £. 40.
			£. s. d.	1st.	2d.	3d.	4th.	5th.	6th.
High-street (a) - -	N.	40	2 8 5½	15	7	11	1	3	4
	S.	58	9 18 10	28	12	10	6	4	2
Chapel-street - -	- -	30	4 6 1	19	6	3	1	- -	1
Vale - - -	- -	28	2 8 4¼	25	- -	1	1	- -	1
Moody-street - -	- -	49	4 11 5¼	32	7	6	3	2	
Bridge-street - -	N.	6	1 10 8½	2	1	2	1	- -	1
(b)	S.	8	– 18 6½	2	4	2			
Little-street (c) - -	- -	5	– 8 7½	2	2	1			
Duck-street (d) - -	N.	9	– 16 4½	5	2	1	1		
	S.	7	– 11 1	4	2	1			
Swan Bank (e) - -	W.	17	1 15 2	7	8	2	1		
	E.	12	2 5 9½	9	1	- -	- -	- -	2
Wag-street - -	E.	21	3 12 5½	18	- -	- -	- -	1	2
	W.	20	1 14 5½	15	3	1	- -	- -	1
Lion-street (f) - -	- -	29	– 13 1½	29					
Wag-lane - - -	W.	16	– 9 1	16					
West-street - -	S.	25	4 8 7½	11	8	2	- -	1	3
	N.	41	1 17 4	33	6	2			
Silk-street (g) - -	- -	27	2 5 1½	24	1	- -	- -	- -	2
Elizabeth-street (h) -	- -	27	– 16 5	27					
Booth-street (i) - -	- -	11	1 19 4	8	- -	1	1	- -	1
West-lane (k) - -	N.	10	4 1 11¾	7	1	- -	- -	1	1
	S.	48	3 9 5	42	1	2	- -	1	2
Marl-field (l) - -	- -	70	3 10 10½	61	5	2	1	- -	1
Dane-street (m) - -	- -	44	1 18 7¼	43	- -	- -	- -	- -	1
Mill-street (n) - -	E.	55	2 11 11½	47	4	2	2		
	W.	88	6 6 10	73	7	2	1	1	4
Mill Green (o) - -	- -	20	4 3 8½	18	- -	1	- -	- -	1
Hill-field (p) - -	- -	45	1 7 4½	42	3				
Rood-lane (q) - -	E.	12	2 11 9	9	- -	- -	2	1	1
	W.	39	1 3 1¼	38	1				
Ryle-street - -	- -	29	2 4 8	26	1	1	- -	- -	1
Stonehouse Green (s) -	- -	44	2 17 –	41	- -	1	- -	- -	2
Buglawton-street -	N.	86	6 3 6¾	73	6	4	- -	- -	3
	S.	36	5 17 2¾	22	5	3	1	- -	5

(a) Or Market Place.
(b) On same line as High-street.
(c) Leading to Bridge-street.
(d) Leading from Bridge-street to Mill-street.
(e) Leading from Mill-street to West street, or upper part of Mill-street.
(f) West side of Wag-street.
(g) South side of West street.
(h) Ditto - - ditto.
(i) Ditto - - ditto.
(k) Continuation of West-street.
(l) South side of West-lane.
(m) North side of West-lane.
(n) Leading to Bridge over River Daven.
(o) East of Macclesfield road.
(p) Ditto - - - ditto.
(q) Or Macclesfield-road.
(r) West side of Macclesfield-road.
(s) East side of Mill-street.

Division of Congleton by the Revising Barristers.

WE have divided the Borough into Three Wards : (that is to say)—The North Ward, the South Ward and the West Ward ; and we have determined and set out the Boundary Line, of each Ward, as follows :—North Ward, from the bottom of Swan Bank, opposite the Bull's Head Inn, to Duck Street ; thence along the Centre of Duck Street, Bridge Streets High Street and Lawton Street ; thence along the Centre of Park Lane to the Boundary of the Borough, near the Village of Biddulph ; thence, Northward, following the Line of the Boundary of the Borough to a Factory belonging to Messrs. Vawdry, and onward, crossing the River Dane, crossing the Road to Macclesfield, crossing the Road to Wilmslow and afterwards crossing the Road to Hulme, Walfield, and so on, continuing the Line of the Boundary of the Borough to the House belonging to Lady Warburton, called Daisy Bank ; thence quitting the Line of Boundary of the Borough across in a straight Line to the Park Gate opening to the top of Rood Lane ; thence down the Centre of Rood Lane over Congleton Bridge, along the Centre of Mill Street to the Point first described opposite the Bull's Head Inn.   This Ward will include the North side of Duck Street, the North side of Bridge Street, the North side of High Street, the North side of Lawton Street, the North side of Park Lane, the East side of Rood Lane, the East side of Mill Street, Bromley Lane, the part of Moss North of Park Lane, the Park, Kinsey Street, Gibraltar, Primrose Vale, Moor Lane, Stonehouse Green, Hill Field and Mill Green.   This Ward will contain 610 rated inhabitants ; the amount of the Rate, 50 l. 13 s. 3 d. ; number of persons rated at 15 l. a year and upwards, 79.   South Ward, from the Point opposite the Lion and Swan Inn in Wag Street, along the Centre of Wag Street and of Wag Lane, until it reaches the Boundary of the Borough at Astbury ; thence, Eastward, following the Line of the Boundary of the Borough to the Village of Biddulph ; thence along the Centre of Park Lane, of Lawton Street, of High Street, of Bridge Street and of Duck Street, up the Centre of Swan Bank to the Point first described, opposite the Lion and Swan Inn.   This Ward will include the East side of Wag Street, the East side of Wag Lane, the South side of Park Lane, the South side of Lawton Street, the South side of High Street, the South side of Bridge Street, the South side of Duck Street, the East side of Swan Bank, the part of Moss South of Park Lane, Little Street, Chapel Street, Moody Street, Vale, Cole Hill and Canal Street. This Ward will contain 485 rated inhabitants ; the amount of the Rate, 48 l. 1 s. 11¾ d. ; number of persons rated at 15 l. a year and upwards, 82.   West Ward, from the Point opposite the Lion and Swan Inn, in Wag Street, Westwardly, along the Centre of Wag Lane across the Sandbach Road to the Boundary of the Borough ; and thence, Northward, following the Line of the Boundary of the Borough, on to the House of Lady Warburton, called Daisy Bank ; thence quitting the Line of the Boundary of the Borough across in a straight Line to the Park Gate, opening to the top of Rood Lane ; thence down the Centre of Rood Lane over Congleton Bridge, along the Centre of Mill Street and Swan Bank to the Point first described, opposite the Lion and Swan Inn.   This Ward will include the West side of Wag Street, the West side of Wag Lane, the West side of Rood Lane, the West side of Mill Street, the West side of Swan Bank, Lion Street, West Street, Silk Street, Elizabeth Street, Booth Street, West Lane, Marlfield, Dane Street, Ryle Street, Cross Ledge, Stoney Lane, Padsbury Lane, West Heath.   This Ward will contain 610 rated inhabitants ; the amount of Rate, 52 l. 19 s. 8¾ d. ; number of persons rated at 15 l. per annum and upwards, 59.   To each of these Wards we have assigned Six Councillors.

Robert Griffiths Temple.

William Charles Townsend.

Approved by His Majesty in Council.

Wm. L. Bathurst.

Borough of Congleton—continued.

NAMES OF STREETS.	Sides of Street.	Number of Inhabited Houses on each side of Street.	Amount of Assessment on each side of Street.	Rate Payers, divided into Six Classes, as below :					
				At and under £. 5.	Above £. 5, up to £. 10.	Above £. 10, up to £. 20.	Above £. 20, up to £. 30.	Above £. 30, up to £. 40.	Above £. 40.
				1st.	2d.	3d.	4th.	5th.	6th.
			£. s. d.						
Moor-lane (ᵃ) -	E.	96	5 13 1½	87	-	4	2	1	2
	W.	41	3 7 4½	31	5	2	2	-	1
Bromley-lane (ᵇ) -	-	25	- 13 7	25	-	-	-	-	-
Primrose Vale (ᶜ) -	-	10	2 1 11	7	-	-	-	-	3
Gibraltar (ᵈ) -	-	42	- 19 11½	41	1	-	-	-	-
Kinsey-street (ᵉ) -	-	39	1 10 - ½	36	2	1	-	-	-
Park (ᶠ) -	-	23	1 13 8	18	3	1	-	-	1
Park-lane -	N.	5	3 4 4	-	1	-	-	2	2
	S.	6	1 11 10¾	-	2	2	-	1	1
Moss Dane Henshaw (ᵍ)	N.	20	6 18 4¾	7	3	3	1	-	6
(ʰ)	S.	78	6 15 11	52	13	7	2	1	3
Cole Hill -	-	22	- 9 4	22	-	-	-	-	-
Canal-street	N.	52	3 1 - ½	42	4	3	1	2	-
	S.	73	1 5 4	73	-	-	-	-	-
Crossledge Bank (ᶦ) -	W.	19	- 12 2½	17	1	1	-	-	-
Stoney-lane (ᵏ) -	E.	9	4 - 11	6	1	-	-	-	2
Padsbury-lane -	-	20	5 19 5	10	-	1	2	3	4
West Heath (ˡ) -	-	19	3 13 - ¾	11	-	4	1	-	3
	-	1,712	151 14 11½	1,358	140	93	34	25	70

(ᵃ) Or Buxton-road.
(ᵇ) Leading to Mills on Dane Henshaw Brook.
(ᶜ) At Bottom of Bromley-lane.
(ᵈ) Ditto   -   ditto.
(ᵉ) Out of North side of High-street.
(ᶠ) From Kinsey-street to Moor-lane.

(ᵍ) North of Leek-road.
(ʰ) South of ditto, on Congleton Edge.
(ᶦ) On London-road, West side.
(ᵏ) East side of London Road, near Ailbury.
(ˡ) Near Padsbury-lane, West of London road.

CONGLETON, DIVIDED INTO THREE WARDS.

NAMES OF WARDS.	Number of Inhabited Houses on each side of Street.	Amount of Assessment.	Rate Payers, divided into Six Classes, as below :					
			At and under £. 5.	Above £. 5, up to £. 10.	Above £. 10, up to £. 20.	Above £. 20, up to £. 30.	Above £. 30, up to £. 40.	Above £. 40.
			1st.	2d.	3d.	4th.	5th.	6th.
		£. s. d.						
Ward No. 1, or Astbury Ward - - -	608	52 19 9	504	44	21	7	7	26
Ward No. 2, or Buglawton Ward * - - -	619	50 12 3½	504	38	33	12	7	27
Ward No. 3, or Canal Ward	485	48 2 11¼	350	58	39	15	11	17
	1,712	151 14 11½	1,358	140	93	34	25	70

* That portion of Buglawton included in the Borough is to be added to the Ward ; it contains about 200 Houses.

ACKNOWLEDGMENTS

The publishers would like to thank the following for their help in the preparation of this book:-

Hilda Kennerley for her generous assistance with our queries concerning the biographical details of Samuel Yates.

Mark Langham of Congleton Library for making his own indexing work of the original book available to us.

Professor David J Parsons for the long loan of his own copy of the original book, also for allowing us to copy relevant sections from his collection of early maps of the area.

PUBLISHER'S NOTE

This book was originally published in Congleton by the author in 1821. Whilst remaining entirely true to the original, and containing reproductions of what are thought to be the author's own drawings, which were hand pasted into his own personal copy, this new Silk Press edition has been completely reset in a modern and more accessible typeface.

The lack of capitalisation and occasionally archaic spelling form part of the charm and quaintness of Samuel Yates's original work which the publisher has sought to retain in this edition. Obvious typographical errors, however, have been corrected.

the Silk Press

the Publishing House for Cheshire, the Moorlands and the Peak

Other limited editions available in this series include:

1

'A Sketch of the Parish of Prestbury'

by George Yamold Osborne

Hard cover, with new illustrations.

750 numbered copies

£23 (Presentation edition in slip case £28.50)

2

'Swythamley and its Neighbourhood'

by Sir Philip Brocklehurst

Hard cover with illustrations from original photographs

500 numbered copies £18.95

3

'Scientific Rambles Round Macclesfield'

by J D Sainter, with an introduction by Alan Garner

Hard cover, newly illustrated.

750 numbered copies £18.95

Also available:

'Views in the High Peaks of Derbyshire'
with an introduction by Mike Langham
Lavishly illustrated, top quality soft cover £5.95

'The Villas of Alderley Edge'
Matthew Hyde
Copiously illustrated, large format
Full colour soft cover £12.95

In preparation:

'Goostrey Remembered'
Due Spring 2000 Price TBA

'Buildings of Knutsford' - a companion volume to
'The Villas of Alderley Edge'
Matthew Hyde
Due Autumn 2000 Price TBA

These titles may be ordered direct from the Publishers at:

The Silk Press, Grosvenor House
45 The Downs, Altrincham, Cheshire WA14 2QG
Telephone: 0161 929 4884 or 0161 928 0333
Fax: 0161 929 8656
Please enclose payment as listed, adding £2.50 for postage and
packing and an extra 75p per volume for multiple orders.